D1205558

MAJOR LEAGUE BASEBALL
MEMORABLE MOMENTS

THE MOST MEMORABLE MOMENTS IN MAJOR LEAGUE BASEBALL® HISTORY

WRITTEN BY KEN LEIKER ● EDITED BY MARK VANCIL

RARE AIR BOOKS

A Division of Rare Air Media

MAJOR LEAGUE BASEBALL MEMORABLE MOMENTS
Created and Produced by Rare Air Books

Copyright © 2002 by Major League Baseball Properties, Inc. All rights reserved.
Compilation © 2002 by Rare Air Media. Text by Ken Leiker, Edited by Mark Vancil
© 2002 Rare Air Media. Produced in partnership with and licensed by Major League
Baseball Properties, Inc. Printed in the United States of America. No part of this book may
be used or reproduced in any manner whatsoever without written permission except in the
case of brief quotations embodied in critical articles and reviews. For information contact
Rare Air Media, PO Box 167393, Chicago, Illinois, 60616-7393.

A Ballantine Book
The Ballantine Publishing Group

All rights reserved under International and Pan-American Copyright Conventions.
Published in the United States by The Ballantine Publishing Group,
a division of Random House, Inc., New York, and simultaneously in Canada
by Random House of Canada Limited, Toronto.

Photography except as noted below © Corbis-Bettman Archives

Jonathan Daniel, *Allsport*	58-59	Otto Greule, *Allsport*	13,117
Elsa Hasch, *Allsport*	30	Harry How, *Allsport*	94
John Iancono, *SI*	56, 106	Walter Iooss Jr., *SI*	110, 112
Jed Jacobsohn, *Allsport*	15, 95	Heinz Kluetmeier, *SI*	55, 69, 126, 129
Ronald C Modra, *SI*	57	Doug Pensinger, *Allsport*	12
Rich Pilling, *MLB photos*	128	Chuck Solomon, *SI*	109
Jamie Squire, *Allsport*	115	Rick Stewart, *Allsport*	114
Michael Zagaris, *MLB photos*	116		

Ballantine and colophon are registered trademarks
of Random House, Inc.

www.ballantinebooks.com

Library of Congress Cataloging-in-Publication Data
can be obtained from the publisher upon request.

ISBN 0-345-46319-6

Manufactured in the United States of America

First Edition: October 2002

10 9 8 7 6 5 4 3 2 1

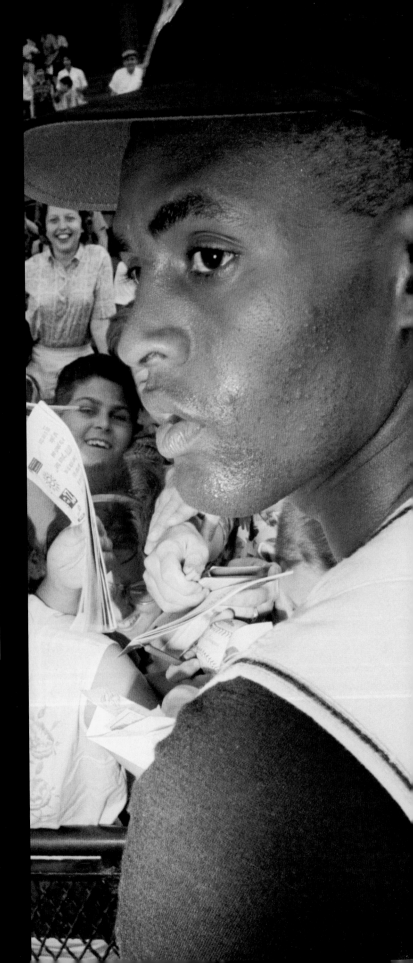

NTRAL ARKANSAS LIBRARY STE
TTLE ROCK PUBLIC LIBRARY
0 ROCK STREET
TTLE ROCK, ARKANSAS 72201

ACKNOWLEDGMENTS

In a summer defined by the creeping shadow of a horrific anniversary and the wire walk leading to baseball's labor agreement, the pages of this book took form. Quietly and without a negative word or intention, so did the wonder and talent of a small group of people whose mark can be found forever imprinted onto the finished product. None of them ever wavered, looked back or questioned the long hours of a process that all the while balanced to one degree or another on factors outside their control.

At Rare Air, Ken Leiker, a trusted friend and remarkable talent, displayed the kind of personal balance and integrity found more often in movies than in real life. His passion, intellect, and character can be found on every page. Nick DeCarlo took an opportunity born of circumstance and without comment or concern grew into a creative force. Moving between a variety of projects while managing the day-to-day for this book, Nick maintained the graphic design integrity that has defined this company's work. As always, John Vieceli's touch can be found inside this book as well. His friendship, work ethic and approach remain invaluable. Paul Sheridan, our counselor and conscience, and Andrew Pipitone are remembered for their friendship, commitment and compassion.

At Major League Baseball, Don Hintze showed yet again the nature and character of a true business partner and friend. In a sports world defined by television and its revenues, Don has quietly become the most innovative print publisher in the business with an attention to detail and an appreciation for quality that extends across all his product lines.

And many thanks to Pete Palmer, a friend and baseball data wizard, who responded to a late plea and 24 hours later provided statistical analysis that enhanced every aspect of the presentation.

As always, the wonder of my life can be found in the beauty, tenderness and love of my wife, Laura, and the incredible, though inexplicable joy born of our girls — Alexandra, Samantha and Isabella Rose. I can imagine nothing more wonderful than the glow of their presence.

Mark Vancil — 2002

To Cherie, James, Nicole, Courtney, Taylor and the angel Bailee — you make all of my moments memorable.

Ken Leiker — 2002

SPECIAL THANKS

To all those at Major League Baseball, particularly Paul Cunningham and Rich Pilling; everybody at Corbis-Bettman, particularly Bill O'Connor and Michael Bacino; Prem Kalliat at *Sports Illustrated;* Howie Burke at Allsport; and Eric Enders at Triple E Productions. Your hard work, quick response and kindness made our work possible.

INTRODUCTION

The game plays every year, across most of a continent, and through parts of three seasons. From the cool and often damp days of April through the heavy heat of August and the falling leaves of October, baseball memories are born splashed with the color of remarkable achievement.

These are moments, events, plays, days, and, in the case of the 2002 Oakland Athletics, weeks. For others such as Barry Bonds, one swing of the bat can provide the context to an entire career. What marks baseball's unique place in the larger cultural experience is the way in which these memories are stored away by a fan base that has no demographic boundaries. For those who watched Don Drysdale and Sandy Koufax in 1965, the incredible dominance of Curt Schilling and Randy Johnson in 2002 recalls and illuminates a place and time nearly 40 years earlier. Was Bonds's 600th home run a memorable moment, or was it the context of Bonds's feat that triggered memories of those old enough to remember Willie Mays and young enough to have cheered for Mark McGwire?

Moments, events, career milestones, seasons of excellence, call them what you will — in the end they represent the collective memory of a game like no other, one that includes parts of three centuries and names like Ruth, DiMaggio, Mays and Aaron whose presence and play has helped define entire decades in America and beyond.

This book provides a glimpse at 30 of the most memorable moments in Major League Baseball history. They

come in all shapes and sizes. Some are electrifying and unpredictable bolts: the home runs by Bobby Thomson, Bill Mazeroski, Carlton Fisk, Kirk Gibson and Joe Carter; "The Catch" by Willie Mays; the ground ball through Bill Buckner's wicket; Luis Gonzalez's bleeder over a drawn-in infield.

Some represent extraordinary individual achievement during the course of a game by the likes of Carl Hubbell, Don Larsen, Reggie Jackson and Jack Morris, Hall of Famers and common folk alike. Some played out over a season or at points in between: Joe DiMaggio's hitting streak, Teddy Ballgame's .406 batting average, Johnny Vander Meer's twin no-hitters,

Matty's World Series whitewashings, Ichiro shrinking the game's international gap. Others are compelling dramas that raised the bar on season home runs, the most glamorous record in baseball, first in 1961 by Roger Maris, then 37 years later by Big Mac and Slammin' Sammy, and again three years after that by Barry Bonds. Some are celebrations of unequalled achievement over the long haul by all-time greats: Roberto Clemente, Hank Aaron, Pete Rose, Rickey Henderson, Nolan Ryan and Cal Ripken Jr.

Some didn't happen between the white lines, but transcended the game: Babe Ruth going to the Yankees, Lou Gehrig saying goodbye. And some are recognition

of Major League Baseball breaking social injustice and doing the right thing: admitting Jackie Robinson and opening the game to all, and acknowledging a baseball treasure named Satchel Paige in the Hall of Fame.

These are just 30 memorable events from among thousands over more than 100 summers of Major League Baseball. Who is to say what is memorable? Baseball, like beauty, is in the eye of the beholder. One fan's cherished memory is another's devastating heartbreak. When Mazeroski hit the home run that ended the 1960 World Series and lifted all of western Pennsylvania into euphoria, a distraught Mickey Mantle sprinted into the clubhouse and spilled his emotion, weeping like a baby. Maz had ruined Mantle's grandest World Series, and Mantle fans everywhere felt his pain. Indeed, these emotional waves have washed over every Major League Baseball city at one time or another in all forms and fashions.

Grand openings like those of Mark "The Bird" Fidrych in 1976, "Super" Joe Charboneau in 1980 and Fernando Valenzuela in 1981 have captivated and invigorated entire cities. In the case of Valenzuela, it

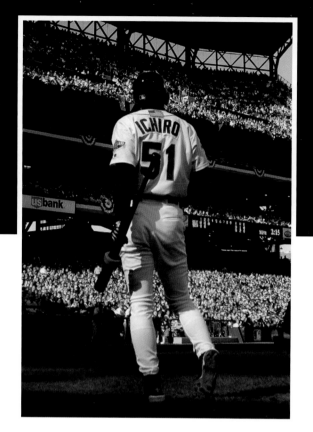

was not only Los Angeles, but also all of Mexico.

And among hundreds of memorable efforts and events, who can deny the wonder of Harvey Haddix pitching 12 perfect innings in 1959 only to lose 1-0 in the 13th; Enos Slaughter's mad dash home in the 1946 World Series; Babe Ruth calling his shot against the Cubs in the 1932 World Series; the Miracle Mets of 1969; or Fred Merkle's "boner" that cost the New York Giants the 1908 NL pennant?

Every season produces memorable moments, and 2002 was no different. The Athletics won 20 consecutive games; Alex Rodriguez set a record for home runs by a shortstop; Bonds joined Mays, Aaron and Ruth as the only players to reach 600 homers; Schilling and Johnson made their case as the most formidable 1-2 pitching duo in history; and Alfonso Soriano sculpted one of the greatest seasons ever by a second baseman.

Each of the 30 memorable moments that spring to life on the following pages captures a place and time. Depending upon your age, location and loyalties, each of them elicits a different memory. In the end, those are feelings that connect generations and in turn define the wonder of baseball.

Mark Vancil and Ken Leiker

★ TABLE OF CONTENTS ★

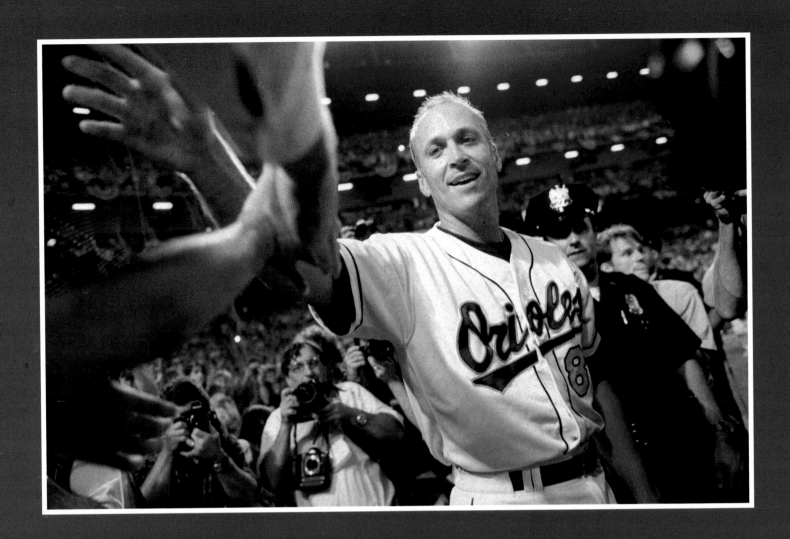

(1995)
CAL RIPKEN JR.
BREAKS LOU GEHRIG'S RECORD FOR CONSECUTIVE GAMES PLAYED

Among the tributes, gifts and accolades afforded Cal Ripken Jr. when he broke Lou Gehrig's 56-year-old record for consecutive games played, one towered above the others, literally and figuratively: the 2,131-pound rock presented by his Baltimore Orioles teammates. Each pound represented a game in Ripken's marvelous streak. The rock itself symbolized the man, for Ripken long since had become Major League Baseball's touchstone for the fans. No common man could identify with McGwire's muscles and moonshots, Ryan's bionic arm and 100-mph gas, Bonds's breathtaking brilliance. The connection was with Ripken, the man who faithfully punched the clock every day for more than 16 years. Sick, injured, hung over, mad at the boss, just feeling lazy — he never called in

sick. As the streak mounted and Ripken was increasingly lauded for his loyalty and dedication to task, every working stiff in America with an exemplary attendance record could swell in the reflected pride and sense of purpose. And Ripken wasn't full of himself, either. He was humble, respectful, self-effacing, every mother's dream for a son, a family man so unaffected by fame he drove his kids to school, a local kid who had realized his dream of playing for the Orioles and never thought about leaving for greater riches in a bigger market.

Just how tightly Ripken had woven into the American fabric became evident on the night that he passed Gehrig. Fans were on the outs with Major League Baseball in 1995, still burned over the players' strike that

12

MOST CONSECUTIVE GAMES PLAYED		FIRST GAME	LAST GAME
CAL RIPKEN JR. BALTIMORE ORIOLES	2,632	MAY 30, 1982	SEPTEMBER 19, 1998
LOU GEHRIG NEW YORK YANKEES	2,130	JUNE 1, 1925	APRIL 30, 1939
EVERETT SCOTT BOSTON RED SOX/NY YANKEES	1,307	JUNE 20, 1916	MAY 5, 1925
STEVE GARVEY LA DODGERS/SD PADRES	1,207	SEPTEMBER 3, 1975	JULY 29, 1983
BILLY WILLIAMS CHICAGO CUBS	1,117	SEPTEMBER 22, 1963	SEPTEMBER 2, 1970
JOE SEWELL CLEVELAND INDIANS	1,103	SEPTEMBER 13, 1922	APRIL 30, 1930
STAN MUSIAL ST. LOUIS CARDINALS	895	APRIL 15, 1952	AUGUST 23, 1957
EDDIE YOST WASHINGTON SENATORS	829	APRIL 30, 1949	MAY 11, 1955
GUS SUHR PITTSBURGH PIRATES	822	SEPTEMBER 11, 1931	JUNE 4, 1937
NELLIE FOX CHICAGO WHITE SOX	798	AUGUST 8, 1955	SEPTEMBER 3, 1960
PETE ROSE CINCINNATI REDS/PHIL PHILLIES	745	SEPTEMBER 2, 1978	AUGUST 23, 1983
DALE MURPHY ATLANTA BRAVES	740	SEPTEMBER 26, 1981	JULY 8, 1986
RICHIE ASHBURN PHILADELPHIA PHILLIES	730	JUNE 7, 1950	APRIL 13, 1955
ERNIE BANKS CHICAGO CUBS	717	AUGUST 28, 1956	JUNE 22, 1961
PETE ROSE CINCINNATI REDS	678	SEPTEMBER 28, 1973	MAY 7, 1978

When it became an official game
in the fifth inning, and Ripken was now the
ALL-TIME IRONMAN OF ALL SPORT,
the crowd rose and cheered as one for more than 22 minutes.

had forced cancellation of the 1994 World Series and delayed the start of the 1995 season. Attendance was down 20 percent, TV ratings were in decline—damn the millionaires on the field and the billionaires in the board room who violated the public trust. Yet fans felt the tug back as Ripken closed in on the record. Oriole Park at Camden Yards was filled on September 6, 1995, and millions more were in front of TV sets for the historic game. When it became an official game in the fifth inning, and Ripken was now the all-time Ironman of all sport, the crowd rose and cheered as one for more than 22 minutes. In ballparks all across America, games were halted as fans and players alike clapped their appreciation for Cal. Ripken knew just how to return the salute. He set out on a lap around the field, shaking hands, high-fiving and small-talking with fans, security guards, grounds workers, old teammates — his constituency all. Once the emotionally charged evening had run its course, hardened hearts

all over the country were softening for baseball again. "I think the game last night and tonight are going to do a lot to help America fall back in love with baseball," remarked President Clinton, who attended the record-breaking event.

Ripken played on unfailingly for three more years. On September 19, 1998, he ducked into Orioles manager Ray Miller's office and said evenly, "Today's the day." The streak finally was frozen at 2,632 games, through 17 seasons, since May 30, 1982. Ripken had grown from a 21-year-old boy into a 38-year-old man, given his best and gotten a lot in return. We have gone this far and have yet to mention that Ripken was an extraordinary ballplayer, one of the best shortstops there ever was, one of only seven men to achieve 3,000 hits and 400 home runs. The numbers are imposing, but the huge rock in Ripken's yard stands for more. Baseball leaned on him, and he bore more than his share.

(1974)

HANK AARON

BREAKS THE ALL-TIME HOME RUN RECORD

Among the great players of his era, Hank Aaron never came in first. He lacked the flair of Mays, the strength of Mantle, the cannon arm of Clemente, the charisma of Banks. He came in when Williams and Musial were still going strong; he left when Jackson and Schmidt were catching their stride. It might have been different had Aaron not played his first 12 seasons in Milwaukee, far from the media glow, long before "Baseball Tonight." As it was, his national stage was limited primarily to two World Series and appearances on "Home Run Derby." When Aaron finally got a national endorsement, a Wheaties commercial in the early 1970s, the script called for him to feign ineptness at both hitting and fielding, a condition that was cured only after he ate his Wheaties.

If the slights bothered Aaron, they never threw him off task. While other ballplayers flashed, crashed and burned out, he kept on his steady way, achieving at a high level — though rarely at the highest level. He was the Major League Baseball leader only once in batting average (.355 in 1959) and only once in home runs (44 in 1957). He never hit more than 47 home runs in a season or accounted for more than 132 RBIs. He hit three home runs in a game only once. Yet day in, day out, year in, year out, Aaron continued his persistent marathon and consistent numbers. When he finally stopped after 23 seasons, he had more home runs, RBIs, total bases and at-bats, and had played in more games, than anyone else in Major League Baseball history.

The home run record had belonged to Babe Ruth and had stood for 39 years. The Babe slammed 714; nobody else had gotten to 600 until Mays

Aaron circled the bases quickly, touched home plate
AND BROKE INTO A GRIN AS BROAD AS ANY THAT HAD BEEN SEEN ON A BALLFIELD.

ALL-TIME HOME RUN LEADERS

1.	HANK AARON	755	9.	MIKE SCHMIDT	548
2.	BABE RUTH	714	10.	MICKEY MANTLE	536
3.	WILLIE MAYS	660	11.	JIMMIE FOXX	534
4.	FRANK ROBINSON	586	12.	WILLIE McCOVEY	521
5.	MARK McGWIRE	583		TED WILLIAMS	521
6.	HARMON KILLEBREW	573	14.	ERNIE BANKS	512
7.	BARRY BONDS	567		EDDIE MATHEWS	512
8.	REGGIE JACKSON	563			

BONDS'S TOTAL IS THROUGH 2001 SEASON

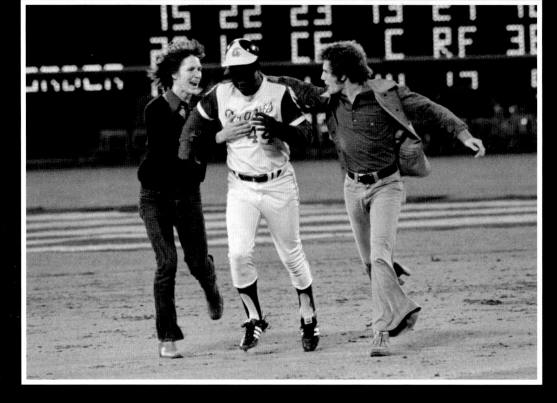

Aaron circled the bases escorted by two exuberant fans and then got a big hug from his mother.

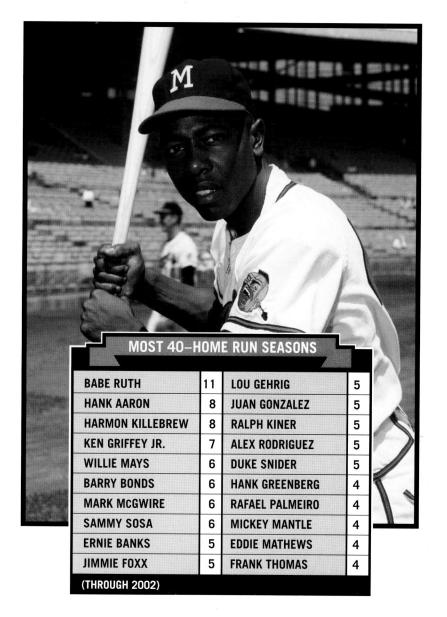

MOST 40–HOME RUN SEASONS			
BABE RUTH	11	LOU GEHRIG	5
HANK AARON	8	JUAN GONZALEZ	5
HARMON KILLEBREW	8	RALPH KINER	5
KEN GRIFFEY JR.	7	ALEX RODRIGUEZ	5
WILLIE MAYS	6	DUKE SNIDER	5
BARRY BONDS	6	HANK GREENBERG	4
MARK McGWIRE	6	RAFAEL PALMEIRO	4
SAMMY SOSA	6	MICKEY MANTLE	4
ERNIE BANKS	5	EDDIE MATHEWS	4
JIMMIE FOXX	5	FRANK THOMAS	4
(THROUGH 2002)			

did in 1969. Aaron was at 398 and 32 years old when the Braves left Milwaukee and took up residence in Atlanta in 1966. He had hit only 56 homers in the previous two seasons, a rate of one every 20.4 at-bats. Yet Atlanta Fulton County Stadium proved to be a hitter-friendly park, "The Launching Pad," and no one enjoyed it more than Aaron, who would average a home run every 13.6 at-bats in an Atlanta uniform. He reached 600 homers in 1971, and when the 1973 season ended he had 713.

Aaron tied Ruth's record in Cincinnati on his first swing of the 1974 season. Four days later, April 8, he still was at 714 when the Braves played their first home game of the season. The Dodgers were in town, and a record crowd of 53,755 was in the stadium. Pearl Bailey sang the National Anthem, Chief Noc-A-Homa held a flaming hoop and per-

formed a tribal dance, and the future president of the United States, Georgia governor Jimmy Carter, was in the house. With the anticipation as thick as the Georgia humidity, Aaron walked in the second inning, then took ball one from Al Downing in the fourth inning. The next pitch came chest-high and true. Aaron whipped his bat around and flicked his powerful wrists — the source of his power — and the ball shot for left field on a climbing arc. It cleared the fence 385 feet from home plate, dropping into the Braves bullpen. Aaron circled the bases quickly, touched home plate and broke into a grin as broad as any that had been seen on a ballfield. At last, he was first — and it was the most celebrated career record in all of sport. The number would grow to 755 before he was done two years later.

(1947)
JACKIE ROBINSON
BREAKS THE COLOR BARRIER

Robinson and Brooklyn Dodgers president Branch Rickey.

"LIFE IS NOT A SPECTATOR SPORT.
If you're going to spend your whole life in the grandstand just watching what goes on,
IN MY OPINION YOU'RE WASTING YOUR LIFE."
— JACKIE ROBINSON

On a sweltering August day in 1945, Branch Rickey paced nervously in his office, awaiting the meeting of a lifetime, a meeting that would alter the course of history. He had been planning this for three years, and now the big moment was about to arrive. Rickey's heart raced when he was informed that Jackie Robinson had arrived. The two men exchanged formalities, then entered Rickey's office and closed the door behind them.

It was a strange pairing for a business meeting of the era — Rickey, a puffy, 63-year-old white man, president of the Brooklyn Dodgers, one of Major League Baseball's most influential franchises; Robinson, a svelte 26-year-old black man, shortstop of the Kansas City Monarchs of the Negro Leagues. Unknown to Robinson, Rickey was bent on inte-

grating Major League Baseball. Rickey's motives were not entirely pristine. He knew in his heart that integration was the right thing to do — but he also was driven by pure capitalism. Before television contracts and corporate sponsors, baseball teams were funded almost exclusively by ticket sales; the better the team, the greater the attendance. Rickey recognized the Negro Leagues as a source of untapped talent for the Dodgers that other teams were unlikely to embrace as quickly. And he knew that integration would widen the fan base, given the Negro Leagues was booming in popularity.

Much was at stake, and it could all go up in smoke if the first black man taken into Major League Baseball in the 20th century wilted under the professional, cultural and social challenges. Rickey in 1942 had briefed

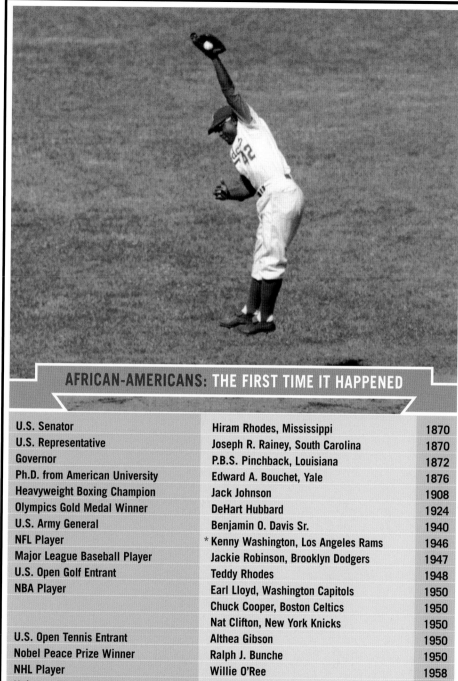

AFRICAN-AMERICANS: THE FIRST TIME IT HAPPENED

U.S. Senator	Hiram Rhodes, Mississippi	1870
U.S. Representative	Joseph R. Rainey, South Carolina	1870
Governor	P.B.S. Pinchback, Louisiana	1872
Ph.D. from American University	Edward A. Bouchet, Yale	1876
Heavyweight Boxing Champion	Jack Johnson	1908
Olympics Gold Medal Winner	DeHart Hubbard	1924
U.S. Army General	Benjamin O. Davis Sr.	1940
NFL Player	* Kenny Washington, Los Angeles Rams	1946
Major League Baseball Player	Jackie Robinson, Brooklyn Dodgers	1947
U.S. Open Golf Entrant	Teddy Rhodes	1948
NBA Player	Earl Lloyd, Washington Capitols	1950
	Chuck Cooper, Boston Celtics	1950
	Nat Clifton, New York Knicks	1950
U.S. Open Tennis Entrant	Althea Gibson	1950
Nobel Peace Prize Winner	Ralph J. Bunche	1950
NHL Player	Willie O'Ree	1958
Heisman Trophy Winner	Ernie Davis, Syracuse	1961
Davis Cup Member	Arthur Ashe	1963
Best Actor Oscar Winner	Sidney Poitier, *Lilies of the Field*	1963
Cabinet Member	Robert C. Weaver	1966
Major League Baseball Umpire	Emmett Ashford	1966
Supreme Court Justice	Thurgood Marshall	1967
Masters Golf Tournament Entrant	Lee Elder	1975
Miss America	Vanessa Williams	1983
Best Actress Oscar Winner	Halle Berry, *Monster's Ball*	2002

* The NFL banned African-Americans in 1933 and didn't admit them again until 1946.

"I'M LOOKING FOR A BALLPLAYER WITH GUTS ENOUGH TO NOT FIGHT BACK."
— BRANCH RICKEY, Brooklyn Dodgers president

"Jackie Robinson was the greatest competitor I've ever seen.
I've seen him beat a team with his bat, his ball, his glove, his feet

◄ ▶, IN A GAME IN CHICAGO ONE TIME, WITH HIS MOUT ◄ ▶

— DUKE SNIDER, Robinson's teammate

scout on the individual he sought, and three years later the scout
him Robinson. He seemed a strange choice, given his reputation
ry temper, combative nature and intolerance to insult. Rickey and
n had no sooner sat down together for the first time when Rickey
bait his visitor by describing racially charged confrontations and
ng to know how Robinson would react to them. Robinson final-
ed. "Do you want a player afraid to fight back?" he shot. Rickey
venly at his guest and spoke his most famous words: "I'm looking
llplayer with guts enough to not fight back." A calm came over
n; as if a light had gone on, he knew what Rickey meant. And
nstantly realized he had found the right man.

Robinson spent 1946 in the minor leagues, and in April 194
on a Brooklyn Dodgers uniform and became the first African-Ame
play Major League Baseball since the late 1800s. Robinson
through insults and indignities, almost always turning the othe
Those who didn't care about the color of his skin quickly grew to
ciate a great ballplayer impassioned to succeed. It was a year
Truman integrated the U.S. military; seven years before the Suprem
ruled segregation in public schools was unconstitutional; eight year
Rosa Parks refused to sit in the back of the bus; 18 years before C
passed the Voting Rights Act. Baseball was a leader in human rig
some social historians mark it as the game's crowning moment.

(1998)

MARK McGWIRE AND SAMMY SOSA

ENGAGE IN A RECORD-SETTING HOME RUN RACE

HEAVY HITTERS

★ ★ ★

The following list ranks the combined total of the top two
home run–hitting players in Major League Baseball every year.
Alex Rodriguez and Sammy Sosa were on pace in 2002 to join the list.

	TOTAL		FIRST		SECOND
2001	137	73	BARRY BONDS	64	SAMMY SOSA
1998	136	70	MARK McGWIRE	66	SAMMY SOSA
1999	128	65	MARK McGWIRE	63	SAMMY SOSA
1961	115	61	ROGER MARIS	54	MICKEY MANTLE
1997	114	58	MARK McGWIRE	56	KEN GRIFFEY JR.
1938	108	58	HANK GREENBERG	50	JIMMIE FOXX
1927	107	60	BABE RUTH	47	LOU GEHRIG
1930	105	56	HACK WILSON	49	BABE RUTH
1947	102	51	JOHNNY MIZE	51	RALPH KINER
1996	102	52	MARK McGWIRE	50	BRADY ANDERSON
1932	99	58	JIMMIE FOXX	41	BABE RUTH
2000	99	50	SAMMY SOSA	49	BARRY BONDS
1955	98	51	WILLIE MAYS	47	TED KLUSZEWSKI
1987	98	49	MARK McGWIRE	49	ANDRE DAWSON
1949	97	54	RALPH KINER	43	TED WILLIAMS
1962	97	49	WILLIE MAYS	48	HARMON KILLEBREW
1969	97	49	HARMON KILLEBREW	48	FRANK HOWARD

McGwire launched No. 62 against Sosa's Cubs.

They had nothing in common, Mark McGwire and Sammy Sosa, two men from starkly contrasting demographics and cultures. What brought them together was the Long Ball. McGwire and Sosa began hitting it so frequently in 1998 that they soon were engaged in a torrid chase for the most hallowed record in sport: 61 home runs in a season, by Roger Maris, 37 years previous. The chase became engrossing drama, played out daily over six months, and hooked much of North America, baseball-loving fans and beyond. The thrill of the chase resonated even greater in the Dominican Republic, the baseball-frenzied Caribbean nation and

McGwire had long been expected to take up the Maris chase. He had blazed into Major League Baseball 11 years earlier, crunching 49 home runs as a rookie. Then he went to work on sculpting his gangly frame into a Bunyan-like physique, found the peace he needed to balance his life, and reached 52 homers in 1996 and 58 a year later. Ken Griffey Jr., too, was expected to take up the Maris chase, having hit 49 and 56 dingers the previous two seasons. Sosa was a surprise entry. He first got to The Show at 20, callow and 50 pounds of muscle short of his prime, didn't dig in for good until 1993, and had not advanced beyond 40 homers in a season

IT WAS FINALLY OVER,
and both men were the victors, richer for the experience and the delightful
MEMORIES THEY CREATED FOR SO MANY.

McGwire set the early pace. He cranked a grand slam on Opening Day, had 11 jacks by the end of April and 27 by the end of May, and tied Reggie Jackson's Major League Baseball record of 37 homers before the All-Star break. Sosa didn't get real until June, when his 20 homers pushed his total to 33. Attention cascaded on the Long Ball warriors. McGwire was stiff at times, affable on occasion, trying hard to be accommodating. Sosa was chatty, oozing exuberance, handling interviews with a twinkle in his eye and an obvious song in his heart — he truly was just happy to be there. One showed the other another way, and they grew to appreciate their differences and developed a fast bond, praising and encouraging each other.

The homers continued to fly. As luck would have it, Sosa's Chicago Cubs were in St. Louis to play McGwire's Cardinals on September 7. McGwire tied Maris that night, and 24 hours later he crashed No. 62. Sosa, who had 58, warmly embraced his huge friend. McGwire saluted the sons and daughters of the late Maris, his guests for the occasion. The chase was over, but the race raged on. Sosa got to 66 homers first, 45 minutes ahead of McGwire. Sammy was done, but Big Mac went deep twice on each of the final two days of the season, raising the bar to 70. It was finally over, and both men were the victors, richer for the experience and the delightful memories they created for so many.

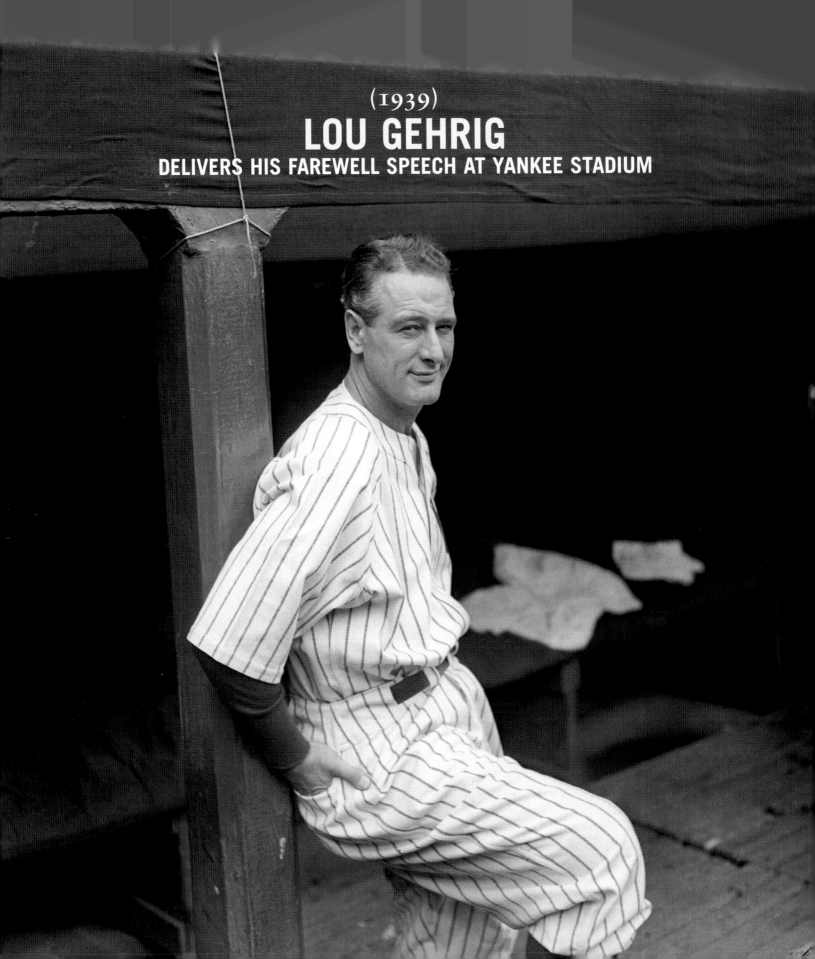

LOU GEHRIG

DELIVERS HIS FAREWELL SPEECH AT YANKEE STADIUM

Few have personified the American Dream like Lou Gehrig did. The son of poor German immigrants, he grew up to be the star first baseman of his hometown New York Yankees, perhaps the best first baseman in history. No matter how rich and famous he became, Gehrig never failed to give his best every day. For 14 years he was as regular as the postman, except the postman got Sunday off and Gehrig didn't. Through it all, he maintained a quiet dignity, never boasting or showing a crass side, never envious of the spotlight dominated by Babe Ruth, his more celebrated teammate. Ruth might be the best ballplayer in history, but he was not the captain of the Yankees. Gehrig was; he engendered that level of respect.

Gehrig's legend began when the Yankees used him as a pinch-hitter on June 1, 1925, and a day later he was playing at first base. The next time he missed a game was May 2, 1939. For 2,130 consecutive games, Gehrig's name appeared in the Yankees boxscore. He played through broken bones, back spasms, concussions and illness. His hands were X-rayed late in his career, and doctors found 17 different fractures that had healed while Gehrig continued to play. In the history of professional sports, only Cal Ripken Jr. has played in more consecutive games than Gehrig had.

Gehrig was a big man for his era, about 6 feet tall, 200 pounds. Naturally strong, he had broad shoulders, a powerful back and massive thighs. Gehrig looked every bit the he-man in the double-breasted suit of the era and even better in the pinstriped uniform of the Yankees. His body, however, began to betray him in spring training 1939. Balls that Gehrig hit right on the screws looped over the infield rather than soar out of the ballpark. His motor skills slipped; he had trouble tying his shoelaces and routine plays at first base required extraordinary effort from him. It got worse after the regular season started, and after eight games Gehrig took himself out of the lineup. He never would play again.

The big man went to the Mayo Clinic in June 1939 and came away

Lou Gehrig's farewell address is among 217 cited in the book *Lend Me Your Ears; Great Speeches in History*, a compendium of classic oratory selected by Pulitzer Prize–winning political columnist William Safire. The only other sports figure included in the collection is baseball executive Branch Rickey for his speech on "The quality that makes a ballplayer great." Here is a list of 12 speeches cited in the chapter "Gallows and Farewell Speeches":

* GREEK PHILOSOPHER SOCRATES, CONDEMNED TO DEATH, ADDRESSES HIS JUDGES.

* KING CHARLES I OF ENGLAND AND, LATER, HIS REGICIDE SPEAK FROM THE SCAFFOLD.

* BRITISH REBEL RICHARD RUMBOLD, ON THE GALLOWS, ATTACKS BOOTED AND SPURRED PRIVILEGE.

* FRENCH REVOLUTIONIST ROBESPIERRE DELIVERS HIS FINAL SPEECH.

* PRESIDENT GEORGE WASHINGTON DELIVERS HIS FAREWELL.

* U.S. ABOLITIONIST JOHN BROWN HAS A FEW WORDS TO SAY ABOUT HIS DEATH SENTENCE.

* KING EDWARD VII OF ENGLAND ABDICATES HIS THRONE.

* NEW YORK YANKEES GREAT LOU GEHRIG BIDS FAREWELL TO BASEBALL.

* GENERAL DOUGLAS MacARTHUR MOVES CONGRESS WITH "OLD SOLDIERS NEVER DIE."

* PRESIDENT DWIGHT EISENHOWER TAKES HIS LEAVE WITH A SURPRISING THEME.

* PRESIDENT LYNDON JOHNSON HALTS THE BOMBING IN VIETNAM AND DROPS HIS OWN POLITICAL BOMB.

* SPEAKER OF THE HOUSE JAMES WRIGHT RESIGNS AS "PROPITIATION" FOR ILL WILL.

with a grim diagnosis: amyotrophic lateral sclerosis, an incurable form of paralysis that destroys the central nervous system and has come to be known as "Lou Gehrig's Disease." He was 36, and he had two years to live.

The story could end right here, and Gehrig would be remembered as one of baseball's greatest treasures. Instead, the chapter that virtually every American has come to know was written on July 4, 1939, Lou Gehrig Appreciation Day at Yankee Stadium. The quiet man stood at home plate and in measured, heart-felt words delivered a message from his soul, the most famous address in baseball history. With dignity and grace, he told more than 60,000 spectators in the stadium and many thousands more listening on the radio: "Today I consider myself the luckiest man on the face of the earth."

Less than two years later, on June 2, 1941, 17 days short of his 38th birthday and 16 years to the day after he replaced Wally Pipp at first base in the Yankees lineup, Gehrig was gone. More than 60 years later, his message remains vibrant:

LIVE EVERY DAY TO YOUR BEST, AND YOUR LIFE WILL BE A CELEBRATION.

The Iron Horse struggled to control his emotions on Lou Gehrig Day.

GEHRIG'S FAREWELL SPEECH

" **FOR THE PAST TWO WEEKS YOU HAVE BEEN READING ABOUT A BAD BREAK. BUT TODAY I CONSIDER MYSELF THE LUCKIEST MAN ON THE FACE OF THE EARTH.**

I have been in ballparks for 17 years and have never received anything but kindness and encouragement from you fans.

Look at these grand men. Which of you wouldn't consider it the highlight of his career just to associate with them for even one day? Sure I'm lucky. Who wouldn't consider it an honor to have known Jacob Ruppert? Also, the builder of baseball's greatest empire, Ed Barrow? To have spent six years with that wonderful little fellow, Miller Huggins? Then to have spent the next nine years with the best manager in baseball today, Joe McCarthy?

Sure I'm lucky. When the New York Giants, a team you would give your right arm to beat, and vice versa, sends you a gift — that's something. When everybody down to the groundskeepers and those boys in white coats remember you with trophies — that's something.

When you have a wonderful mother-in-law who takes sides with you in squabbles with her own daughter — that's something. When you have a father and a mother who work all their lives so you can have an education and build your body — it's a blessing. When you have a wife who has been a tower of strength and shown more courage than you dreamed existed — that's the finest I know.

I MIGHT HAVE BEEN GIVEN A BAD BREAK, BUT I'VE GOT AN AWFUL LOT TO LIVE FOR. THANK YOU. "

(1941)
TED WILLIAMS
HITS .406 — THE LAST PLAYER TO ACHIEVE .400

"If I was being paid $30,000 a year, THE VERY LEAST I COULD DO WAS HIT .400."

T he major leagues had not seen a .400 hitter in 11 years when Ted Williams arrived at the final day of the 1941 season with a .39955 batting average. The talk of the day was that if he sat out the doubleheader in Philadelphia, Williams would have his .400 season, since the .39955 would have been rounded up to .400. Ever the perfectionist, Williams would have none of it. For him, the chasm between .39955 and .400 was the breadth of the Grand Canyon.

Williams's day of reckoning had arrived in his 23rd year, just his third in the major leagues. He had been born for this. From as early as he could remember, his life had been consumed by the art of hitting a baseball. He wasn't shy about saying that he meant to become "the greatest hitter who ever lived," and he thrust all of his being into achieving that goal.

As a child, when everyone else was sleeping, Williams was in his backyard alone, swinging a bat over and over and over. He never could get in enough swings. Even after he became a star in the big leagues, he would

"DID THEY TELL ME HOW TO PITCH TO WILLIAMS?

Sure they did. It was great advice, very encouraging. They said he had no weakness,
won't swing at a bad ball, has the best eyes in the business,
and can kill you with one swing. He won't hit anything bad,

BUT DON'T GIVE HIM ANYTHING GOOD."

— BOBBY SHANTZ, Major League Baseball player, 1949–1964

abruptly get out of bed during the night, summoned by his insatiable dedication, and swing whatever was handy, a rolled-up newspaper, a pillow, a shoe. Those who knew him joked that if he had doted on any of his three wives as much as he did on his bats, he might have had a marriage that lasted. He didn't drink or smoke, always was in by curfew, and at one point quit going to movies for fear that watching in the dark might damage his rare 20/10 eyesight — all in the name of hitting a baseball harder, farther and more frequently than anyone else.

When Sunday, September 28, 1941, dawned, Williams was ready to cross the threshold into greatness; he had been preparing for a lifetime.

The mere mortals pitching for the Philadelphia Athletics that afternoon had no chance to keep .39955 at bay. Before Williams dug in for his first at-bat, umpire Bill McGowan bent over and dusted off home plate. Without looking up, McGowan said, "To hit .400, a batter has got to be loose." Teddy Ballgame nodded his agreement, then proceeded to drive baseballs all over Shibe Park, including one that landed on 20th Street beyond the right-field wall, some 440 feet from home plate, for his 37th home run of the season. When his day's work was done, Williams had six hits in eight at-bats and a .406 average, rounded up from .4057. More than 60 years later, no one has drawn closer to that mark than .394.

TED WILLIAMS'S 1941 SEASON, MONTH BY MONTH

	AB	R	H	HR	RBI	BB	SO	BA
APRIL	18	3	7	1	5	1	1	.389
MAY	101	29	44	6	22	22	3	.436
JUNE	94	33	35	8	29	30	5	.372
JULY	63	20	27	6	19	16	5	.429
AUGUST	107	31	43	10	26	50	8	.402
SEPTEMBER	73	19	29	6	19	26	5	.397
SEASON	456	135	185	37	120	145	27	.406

"They can talk about Babe Ruth and Ty Cobb and Rogers Hornsby and Lou Gehrig and Joe DiMaggio and Stan Musial and all the rest, but I'm sure not one of them could hold cards and spades to Ted Williams in his sheer knowledge of hitting. He studied hitting the way a broker studies the stock market, and could spot at a glance mistakes that others couldn't see in a week."

— CARL YASTRZEMSKI, Major League Baseball player, 1961–1983

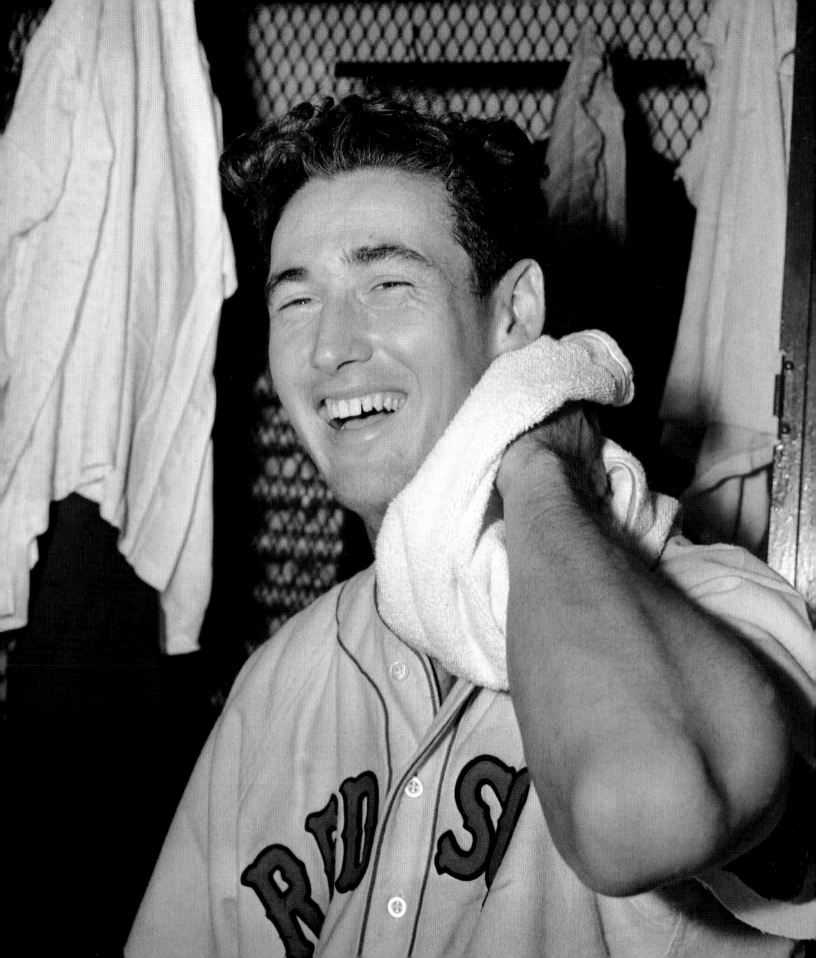

RULES ARE MADE TO BE BROKEN

★ ★ ★

If Ted Williams had been playing by today's rules, his 1941 batting average would have been .411 instead of .406. In today's game, a sacrifice fly does not count as a time at-bat, but that was not the case in 1941. Following is a list of the highest batting averages since 1941 and what they would have been under 1941 rules.

PLAYER	YR	BA	1941 BA
TONY GWYNN	1994	.394	.389
GEORGE BRETT	1980	.390	.384
ROD CAREW	1977	.388	.385
TED WILLIAMS	1957	.388	.386
LARRY WALKER	1999	.379	.374
STAN MUSIAL	1948	.376	.376
THROUGH 2001 SEASON			

BEST BATTING AVERAGES SINCE 1941

TONY GWYNN SAN DIEGO PADRES	1994	.394
GEORGE BRETT KANSAS CITY ROYALS	1980	.390
TED WILLIAMS BOSTON RED SOX	1957	.388
ROD CAREW MINNESOTA TWINS	1977	.388
LARRY WALKER COLORADO ROCKIES	1999	.379
STAN MUSIAL ST. LOUIS CARDINALS	1948	.376
TONY GWYNN SAN DIEGO PADRES	1997	.372
NOMAR GARCIAPARRA BOSTON RED SOX	2000	.372
TODD HELTON COLORADO ROCKIES	2000	.372
TONY GWYNN SAN DIEGO PADRES	1987	.370
ANDRES GALARRAGA COLORADO ROCKIES	1993	.370

THROUGH 2001 SEASON

"A man has to have goals — for a day, for a lifetime —
and that was mine, to have people say, 'There goes Ted Williams,

THE GREATEST HITTER WHO EVER LIVED.' "

(1985)
PETE ROSE
BREAKS TY COBB'S ALL-TIME RECORD FOR HITS

Whatever his transgressions against Major League Baseball, Pete Rose remains among the purest ballplayers of all time. His gift to the game was exceedingly generous: All he had in him, he left on the field, every time he played, no regrets for him, no complaints for those who watched. Nobody can say they loved baseball more than Rose did, for it couldn't possibly be true.

In physical appearance, he was just one of the crowd, ordinary, not even 6 feet in stature. He didn't measure up in size, strength, speed or arm power to many that played on the same field. Rose certainly was the least imposing among the vital cogs of Cincinnati's Big Red Machine of the 1970s, yet crowd appreciation for Rose always seemed a little greater than it was for Bench, Morgan, Perez or Foster. Rose was a hometown boy, born and raised in Cincinnati, and the people in the seats recognized and honored a common man on the field who beat the real athletes through determination, dedica-

MOST HITS AFTER 35TH BIRTHDAY

PETE ROSE	1,698
SAM RICE	1,574
HONUS WAGNER	1,288
PAUL MOLITOR	1,285
CARL YASTRZEMSKI	1,179
TY COBB	1,136
CARLTON FISK	1,043
NAP LAJOIE	1,040
DOC CRAMER	1,035
STAN MUSIAL	1,033
DAVE WINFIELD	1,027
LUKE APPLING	1,023
HANK AARON	979
LAVE CROSS	966
JAKE DAUBERT	939
TRIS SPEAKER	938

Doesn't include 19th-century players

As with all driven men, Rose was selfish. He wanted for himself the record that defined what he did best:

THE MOST HITS IN MAJOR LEAGUE BASEBALL HISTORY,
a record seemingly cast in granite when Ty Cobb retired in 1928 with 4,191.

tion and sheer will. Rose hit singles and hustled them into doubles, forever a headfirst blur. He crashed into catchers in full gear with the force of a linebacker. He couldn't hold a regular position, yet was in the All-Star Game starting lineup as a first baseman, second baseman, third baseman, leftfielder and rightfielder — a feat no one else has come close to achieving.

As with all driven men, Rose was selfish. He wanted for himself the record that defined what he did best: the most hits in Major League Baseball history, a record seemingly cast in granite when Ty Cobb retired in 1928 with 4,191. Asked once what the inscription on his tombstone should say, Rose shot back without hesitation: "Here lies the man who could hit forever." Rose's single-minded purpose melded well in the team game. So well, in fact, that when his career was over, he had played on the winning side in more games than anyone else in team sports history.

The hits came regularly for Rose even as he passed his 40th birthday and had enough gray hair to procure a commercial endorsement for hair coloring. Finally, on September 11, 1985, the 44-year-old Rose approached the left side of home plate in the first inning at Cincinnati's Riverfront Stadium, dropped into his familiar exaggerated crouch and waited to see what Eric Show had to offer. Show's third pitch came knee-high and on the outside part of the plate. As he had done thousands of times previously, Rose took a measured swing, connected solidly and drove the ball into left-center field. It skipped onto the artificial turf at 8:01 p.m. As always, Rose rounded first base on the fly, alert for any defensive glitch that would enable him to bolt for second. Satisfied he could go no farther, Rose pushed his helmet down on his head in another familiar mannerism and retreated to first base. He had achieved 4,192.

Rose would stretch the number to 4,256 before he finished playing in 1986, his 24th season. He didn't play forever or hit forever, but he was in more games and had more hits than any other man in Major League Baseball history. He is the Hit King, and nobody else can fairly have that as their epitaph.

ALL-TIME HITS LEADERS

#	Player	Hits	#	Player	Hits
1.	PETE ROSE	4,256	9.	PAUL MOLITOR	3,319
2.	TY COBB	4,189	10.	EDDIE COLLINS	3,315
3.	HANK AARON	3,771	11.	WILLIE MAYS	3,283
4.	STAN MUSIAL	3,630	12.	EDDIE MURRAY	3,255
5.	TRIS SPEAKER	3,514	13.	NAP LAJOIE	3,242
6.	CARL YASTRZEMSKI	3,419	14.	CAL RIPKEN JR.	3,184
7.	CAP ANSON	3,418	15.	GEORGE BRETT	3,154
8.	HONUS WAGNER	3,415	16.	PAUL WANER	3,152

Research done after 1985 concluded that Cobb's total was 4,189, not 4,191, which is what it was believed to be when Rose surpassed Cobb.

(1941)
JOE DiMAGGIO
HITS SAFELY IN 56 CONSECUTIVE GAMES

"DiMaggio was the greatest all-around player I ever saw.

HIS CAREER CANNOT BE SUMMED UP IN NUMBERS AND AWARDS.

It might sound corny, but he had a profound and lasting impact on the country."

— TED WILLIAMS

America never has been riveted to baseball quite like it was for two months in the summer of 1941. It was an unsettling time in the world, the uneasy calm before the storm. Hitler and the Nazis ruled Germany and were plotting to take the rest of Europe. The Japanese were the silent enemy across the Pacific. President Roosevelt challenged Congress to prepare for national defense. The American public needed respite from the grim news of the real world and found it in a sporting drama that became more gripping with each passing day. "Did he get a hit?" became the most popular refrain in the country.

Joe DiMaggio, the gifted and graceful centerfielder of the mighty New York Yankees, was getting a hit every day. Starting on May 15 and winding through June and into July, DiMaggio hit safely in 56 consecutive games, a streak that many regard as the most remarkable achievement in sports history. Consider that more than 60 years have passed since DiMaggio's feat, and no one has come closer than 44 games. That's still 20 percent short, two weeks' worth of games.

DiMaggio's streak was the signature achievement of his sterling career, yet it served to measure him more as an American icon than a ballplayer, broadening an audience that was mesmerized by his excellence, elegance and charisma. Except for Babe Ruth, no ballplayer has ever captivated and fascinated the American public like DiMaggio did. He was poised, confident, proud, humble, detached, seemingly above human frailties. He rarely showed emotion on the field, reacting to success and failure in the same stoic manner. Baseball contemporaries spoke of him in reverent tones. Hemingway wrote of "the great DiMaggio" in *The Old Man and the Sea*. After he left baseball, DiMaggio married Marilyn Monroe, the world's most glamorous woman. When Major League Baseball celebrated the 100th anniversary of professional baseball in 1969, DiMaggio was voted the "Greatest Living Player." Even if he wasn't, he was — his legend was that awe-inspiring. DiMaggio never disappointed his adoring public, yet he was a private man who left much unsaid, which only added to the mystique about him. For years, the most coveted autobiography among book publishers was DiMaggio's, but he refused all offers, taking his innermost thoughts with him to the grave in 1999.

DiMaggio was performing like a common ballplayer before launching his 1941 hitting streak on May 15, batting only .306 after batting-championship seasons of .381 in 1939 and .352 in 1940. He had few close calls in the streak, needing a hit in his final at-bat only a few times. When pitchers became loathe to throw DiMaggio strikes, Yankees manager Joe McCarthy allowed him to swing away on 3-and-0 counts. DiMaggio had a .408 batting average (91 for 223), 15 homers and 55 RBIs during the streak, and after it ended he had a hit in each of the next 16 games, meaning he had hit safely in 72 of 73 games.

The 56-game streak ended on July 17 in Cleveland, in front of a crowd of more than 67,000. Indians third baseman Ken Keltner twice robbed DiMaggio of hits. In his final at-bat, DiMaggio sent a hard grounder to the left side that kicked up late, but shortstop Lou Boudreau was able to snatch the ball near his shoulder and flip to second baseman Ray Mack in time to start a double play. Befitting his image, DiMaggio showed no emotion.

DiMaggio's streak was the signature achievement of his sterling career, yet it served to measure him

MORE AS AN AMERICAN ICON THAN A BALLPLAYER,

broadening an audience that was mesmerized by his excellence, elegance and charisma.

It's over. DiMaggio made zeros with his fingers and flashed a weary grin after failing to get a hit for the first time in 57 games.

JOE DiMAGGIO'S HITTING STREAK

DATE/OPPONENT	AB	R	H	2B	3B	HR	RBI
MAY 15 CHICAGO	4	0	1	0	0	0	1
MAY 16 CHICAGO	4	2	2	0	1	1	1
MAY 17 CHICAGO	3	1	1	0	0	0	0
MAY 18 ST. LOUIS	3	3	3	1	0	0	1
MAY 19 ST. LOUIS	3	0	1	1	0	0	0
MAY 20 ST. LOUIS	5	1	1	0	0	0	1
MAY 21 DETROIT	5	0	2	0	0	0	1
MAY 22 DETROIT	4	0	1	0	0	0	1
MAY 23 BOSTON	5	0	1	0	0	0	2
MAY 24 BOSTON	4	2	1	0	0	0	2
MAY 25 BOSTON	4	0	1	0	0	0	0
MAY 27 at WASHINGTON	5	3	4	0	0	1	3
MAY 28 at WASHINGTON	4	1	1	0	1	0	0
MAY 29 at WASHINGTON	3	1	1	0	0	0	0
MAY 30 at BOSTON	2	1	1	0	0	0	0
MAY 30 at BOSTON	3	0	1	1	0	0	0

DATE/OPPONENT	AB	R	H	2B	3B	HR	RBI
JUNE 1 at CLEVELAND	4	1	1	0	0	0	0
JUNE 1 at CLEVELAND	4	0	1	0	0	0	0
JUNE 2 at CLEVELAND	4	2	2	1	0	0	0
JUNE 3 at DETROIT	4	1	1	0	0	1	1
JUNE 5 at DETROIT	5	1	1	0	1	0	1
JUNE 7 at ST. LOUIS	5	2	3	0	0	0	1
JUNE 8 at ST. LOUIS	4	3	2	0	0	2	4
JUNE 8 at ST. LOUIS	4	1	2	1	0	1	3
JUNE 10 at CHICAGO	5	1	1	0	0	0	0
JUNE 12 at CHICAGO	4	1	2	0	0	1	1
JUNE 14 CLEVELAND	2	0	1	1	0	0	1
JUNE 15 CLEVELAND	3	1	1	0	0	1	1
JUNE 16 CLEVELAND	5	0	1	1	0	0	0
JUNE 17 CHICAGO	4	1	1	0	0	0	0
JUNE 18 CHICAGO	3	0	1	0	0	0	0
JUNE 19 CHICAGO	3	2	3	0	0	1	2
JUNE 20 DETROIT	5	3	4	1	0	0	1
JUNE 21 DETROIT	4	0	1	0	0	0	0
JUNE 22 DETROIT	5	1	2	1	0	1	2
JUNE 24 ST. LOUIS	4	1	1	0	0	0	0
JUNE 25 ST. LOUIS	4	1	1	0	0	0	0
JUNE 26 ST. LOUIS	4	0	1	1	0	0	1
JUNE 27 at PHILADELPHIA	3	1	2	0	0	1	2
JUNE 28 at PHILADELPHIA	5	1	2	1	0	0	0
JUNE 29 at WASHINGTON	4	1	1	1	0	0	0
JUNE 29 at WASHINGTON	5	1	1	0	0	0	1

DATE/OPPONENT	AB	R	H	2B	3B	HR	RBI
JULY 1 BOSTON	4	0	2	0	0	0	1
JULY 1 BOSTON	3	1	1	0	0	0	0
JULY 2 BOSTON	5	1	1	0	0	1	3
JULY 5 PHILADELPHIA	4	2	1	0	0	1	2
JULY 6 PHILADELPHIA	5	2	4	1	0	0	2
JULY 6 PHILADELPHIA	4	0	2	0	1	0	2
JULY 10 at ST. LOUIS	2	0	1	0	0	0	0
JULY 11 at ST. LOUIS	5	1	4	0	0	1	2
JULY 12 at ST. LOUIS	5	1	2	1	0	0	1
JULY 13 at CHICAGO	4	2	3	0	0	0	0
JULY 13 at CHICAGO	4	0	1	0	0	0	0
JULY 14 at CHICAGO	3	0	1	0	0	0	0
JULY 15 at CHICAGO	4	1	2	1	0	0	2
JULY 16 at CLEVELAND	4	3	3	1	0	0	0
TOTALS	223	56	91	16	4	15	55

Longest Hitting Streaks

PLAYER	YR	TEAM	G	PLAYER	YR	TEAM	G	PLAYER	YR	TEAM	G
Joe DiMaggio	1941	New York (AL)	56	George McQuinn	1938	St. Louis (AL)	34	Vladimir Guerrero	1999	Montreal	31
Willie Keeler	1897	Baltimore (NL)	44	Dom DiMaggio	1949	Boston (AL)	34	Cal McVey	1876	Chicago (NL)	30
Pete Rose	1978	Cincinnati	44	Benito Santiago	1987	San Diego	34	Elmer Smith	1898	Cincinnati	30
Bill Dahlen	1894	Chicago (NL)	42	George Davis	1893	New York (NL)	33	Tris Speaker	1912	Boston (AL)	30
George Sisler	1922	St. Louis (AL)	41	Hal Chase	1907	New York (AL)	33	Goose Goslin	1934	Detroit	30
Ty Cobb	1911	Detroit	40	Rogers Hornsby	1922	St. Louis (NL)	33	Stan Musial	1950	St. Louis (NL)	30
Paul Molitor	1987	Milwaukee (AL)	39	Heinie Manush	1933	Washington	33	Ron LeFlore	1976	Detroit	30
Tommy Holmes	1945	Boston (NL)	37	Ed Delahanty	1899	Philadelphia (NL)	31	George Brett	1980	Kansas City	30
Billy Hamilton	1894	Philadelphia (NL)	36	Nap Lajoie	1906	Cleveland	31	Jerome Walton	1989	Chicago (NL)	30
Fred Clarke	1895	Louisville (NL)	35	Sam Rice	1924	Washington	31	Nomar Garciaparra	1997	Boston (AL)	30
Ty Cobb	1917	Detroit	35	Willie Davis	1969	Los Angeles	31	Sandy Alomar Jr.	1997	Cleveland	30
Luis Castillo	2002	Florida	35	Rico Carty	1970	Atlanta	31	Eric Davis	1998	Baltimore	30
George Sisler	1925	St. Louis (AL)	34	Ken Landreaux	1980	Minnesota	31	Luis Gonzalez	1999	Arizona	30

(1988)
KIRK GIBSON
ENDS GAME 1 OF THE WORLD SERIES WITH A HOME RUN

T he balmy calm of spring training came to an abrupt halt in Vero Beach, Florida. Someone had pulled a prank on the newest member of the Los Angeles Dodgers, smearing eye black on the inside of his baseball cap. When Kirk Gibson pulled that cap onto his head on March 3, 1988, he had his game-face on, ready for the first exhibition of the Grapefruit League season. The Dodgers soon would learn that Gibson always wore his game-face. Upon discovering the black substance that had transferred to his forehead, Gibson flew into a rage that had teammates trembling and scurrying. He questioned whether he could coexist with play-babies who didn't respect the sanctity of the workplace, cursed the blasé culture that he perceived to be rampant on the team, then stormed out of the building before he really snapped and wrung someone's neck.

Though Gibson was a remarkably gifted athlete, tall, sleek and chiseled, baseball did not come naturally for him. His swing was a grunt and a hack, rather than the fluid, supple motion of a pure hitter. He could catch a fly ball hit his way, but was unsteady and often stumbled if he had to track it very far. His arm strength? Gibson's manager in Detroit, Sparky Anderson, glumly put it best: "It's always going to happen: Runners just go from first to third on almost every ball hit out there." Gibson was a career .268 hitter, never had more than 29 home runs or 97 RBIs in a season, never played in an All-Star Game. Yet this is a man that every Major League Baseball team wanted in its lineup — or, as they say in football, wanted to go to war with. Gibson had been a great football player, stoked by raw intensity and fierce competitiveness, and he merely transferred those qualities to the baseball diamond. With his three-day stubble and menacing scowl, he looked the part and backed it up, too.

The 1987 Dodgers were a soft team, 16 games under .500. They played, they lost, they went home, nobody kicking over the water cooler,

PINCH-HIT HOME RUNS IN THE WORLD SERIES

PLAYER	SERIES	G	SITUATION	SCORE	PLAYER	SERIES	G	SITUATION	SCORE
JIM LEYRITZ NEW YORK (AL)	1999	4	8TH IN, NONE ON	W, 4-1	**ELSTON HOWARD** NEW YORK (AL)	1960	1	9TH IN, ONE ON	L, 6-4
ED SPRAGUE TORONTO	1992	2	9TH IN, ONE ON	W, 5-4	**CHUCK ESSEGIAN** LOS ANGELES	1959	6	9TH IN, NONE ON	W, 9-3
CHILI DAVIS MINNESOTA	1991	3	8TH IN, ONE ON	* L, 5-4	**CHUCK ESSEGIAN** LOS ANGELES	1959	2	7TH IN, NONE ON	W, 4-3
BILL BATHE SAN FRANCISCO	1989	3	9TH IN, TWO ON	L, 13-7	**BOB CERV,** NEW YORK (AL)	1955	5	7TH IN, NONE ON	L, 5-3
KIRK GIBSON LOS ANGELES	1988	1	9TH IN, ONE ON	W, 5-4	**HANK MAJESKI** CLEVELAND	1954	4	5TH IN, TWO ON	L, 7-4
JAY JOHNSTONE LOS ANGELES	1981	4	6TH IN, ONE ON	W, 8-7	**DUSTY RHODES** NEW YORK (NL)	1954	1	10TH IN, TWO ON	W, 5-2
BERNIE CARBO BOSTON	1975	6	8TH IN, TWO ON	* W, 7-6	**GEORGE SHUBA** BROOKLYN	1953	1	6TH IN, ONE ON	L, 9-5
BERNIE CARBO BOSTON	1975	3	7TH IN, NONE ON	L, 6-5	**JOHNNY MIZE,** NEW YORK (AL)	1952	3	9TH IN, NONE ON	L, 5-3
JOHN BLANCHARD NEW YORK (AL)	1961	3	8TH IN, NONE ON	W, 3-2	**YOGI BERRA,** NEW YORK (AL)	1947	3	7TH IN, NONE ON	L, 9-8

* 12 INNINGS

Gibson returned to the bench for the final four games. The Dodgers didn't need him;
HE HAD TAUGHT THEM ALL THEY NEEDED TO KNOW.

tearing up the clubhouse, or upbraiding the malingerers. When Gibson hit the free-agent market after the season, the Dodgers knew he was just the jolt they needed. The front office signed him, then turned him loose on the lambs in Dodger blue. Gibson set the rules with his spring-training tirade and before long the whole team had taken on his toughness, no one more than Orel Hershiser, the "Bulldog," who went 23-8 and in one remarkable stretch pitched a record 59 consecutive shutout innings. The Dodgers soared to the National League pennant, despite no .300 hitters, no 30-homer men, no 100-RBI producers. Gibson from a statistics standpoint (.290, 25 home runs, 76 RBIs, 31 stolen bases) had one of the weakest league MVP seasons in history, but the numbers hardly told the story. This ballplayer's special traits became evident to all in the first game of the World Series. He carved his niche in baseball lore that night in Dodger Stadium.

Gibson rarely made it through a season without grinding his body to a pulp, and this time it was his hamstring and knee that were so sore he probably wasn't going to be able to play against the powerful Oakland Athletics. The Dodgers trailed 4-3 into the last of the ninth, and the great Dennis Eckersley, the game's premier relief pitcher, got two outs before walking a batter. Lo and behold, that was Gibson limping out of the dugout to pinch-hit, the crowd roaring louder with each of his gimps to the plate. Gibson meekly fouled off two pitches, worked the count full, then choked up on his bat and set his jaw. Eckersley delivered a slider that failed to break, and Gibson sent it on a soaring line into the right-field seats. The Dodgers had a stunning 5-4 victory. As he circled the bases gingerly, Gibson pumped his right arm furiously at his side and allowed a wide grin to crack his game-face. The heavily favored A's never recovered, losing the Series in five games. Gibson returned to the bench for the final four games. The Dodgers didn't need him; he had taught them all they needed to know.

(1991)
NOLAN RYAN
PITCHES HIS SEVENTH NO-HITTER, THREE MORE THAN ANYONE ELSE

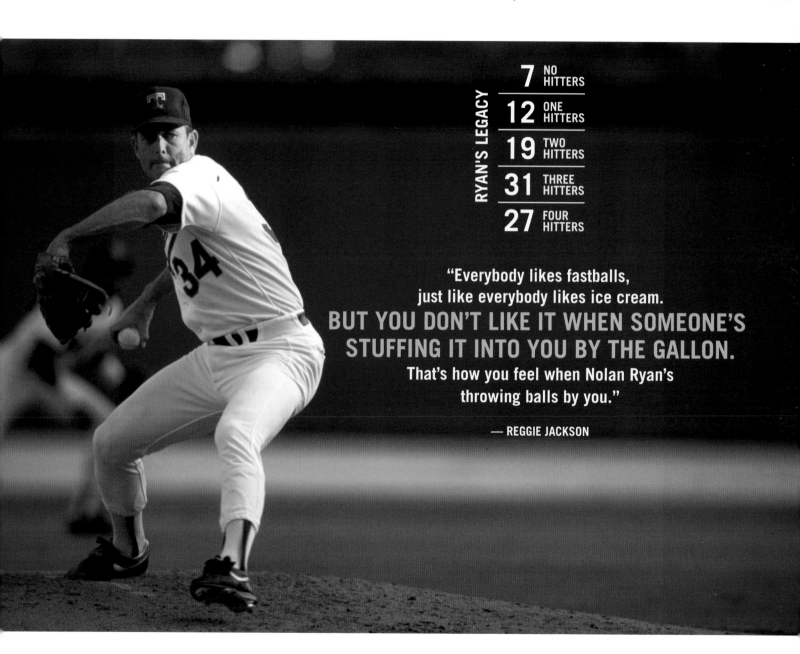

RYAN'S LEGACY

7	NO HITTERS
12	ONE HITTERS
19	TWO HITTERS
31	THREE HITTERS
27	FOUR HITTERS

"Everybody likes fastballs,
just like everybody likes ice cream.
**BUT YOU DON'T LIKE IT WHEN SOMEONE'S
STUFFING IT INTO YOU BY THE GALLON.**
That's how you feel when Nolan Ryan's
throwing balls by you."

— REGGIE JACKSON

IT WAS ALMOST 12

In addition to his seven no-hitters, Nolan Ryan had not yielded a hit after eight innings in five games. Each time he settled for a one hitter. Ryan's no-hit bids that ended in the ninth inning:

AUGUST 7, 1974	DICK ALLEN CHICAGO WHITE SOX	ONE-OUT SINGLE
JULY 13, 1979	REGGIE JACKSON NEW YORK YANKEES	ONE-OUT SINGLE
APRIL 27, 1988	MIKE SCHMIDT PHILADELPHIA PHILLIES	ONE-OUT SINGLE
APRIL 23, 1989	NELSON LIRIANO TORONTO BLUE JAYS	ONE-OUT TRIPLE
AUGUST 10, 1989	DAVE BERGMAN DETROIT TIGERS	ONE-OUT SINGLE

He was a John Wayne–type character, born and bred a Texan, tall, raw-boned and straight as a board, respectful of his elders, unwaveringly polite unless provoked. Nolan Ryan threw a baseball as fast as any man who ever lived and humbled some of Major League Baseball's greatest hitters, yet that was only part of his legacy. He represented hard work, fair play, clean living and humility. Kids idolized him. Parents held him up as a role model. When Ryan played for the Texas Rangers, the team once invited anyone named Nolan or Ryan onto the field at Arlington Stadium for a parade. More than 1,000 kids participated with their beaming parents watching.

Even larger than the fraternity of those named after Ryan is the club populated by men whom Ryan struck out. Anyone who played Major

League Baseball between 1966 and 1993 and does not belong to that group was probably in whichever league Ryan wasn't in; was an American League pitcher and had the designated hitter bat in his place; or was able to beg out of the lineup by excuse of injury or illness, often feigned, when Ryan was pitching. Respect for Ryan ran so high that some players, dropped all pretensions and admitted their team was better off with them on the bench when Ryan was on the mound.

For 27 seasons, batters approached home plate to face Ryan as if walking to the gallows. Before his remarkable right arm finally dropped limp on September 22, 1993 on the Seattle Kingdome's mound, 5,714 batters became Ryan's strikeout victims. He recorded 28 percent more strikeouts than any other pitcher in history, twice as many as all but 11

★ ★ ★ ★ ★

ALL IN THE FAMILY
**Nolan Ryan struck out
the following fathers and sons.**

FATHER	SON
SANDY ALOMAR SR.	ROBERTO ALOMAR
	SANDY ALOMAR JR.
BOBBY BONDS	BARRY BONDS
TITO FRANCONA	TERRY FRANCONA
KEN GRIFFEY SR.	KEN GRIFFEY JR.
HAL McRAE	BRIAN McRAE
DICK SCHOFIELD SR.	DICK SCHOFIELD JR.
MAURY WILLS	BUMP WILLS

rs in history. Among the top
seasons for strikeouts, Ryan
383) and fourth (367). He K'd
rent players, including seven
generation later, their sons, and
others. He fanned 27 who later
Hall of Fame; whiffed every
ing of the last quarter-century:
n, McGwire, Bonds.
se days when he had control of
cking curveball to complement
00-mph fastball, Ryan was as close to being unhittable as any
ever been. At 26, he pitched two no-hitters, then another in
next two years. At 34, he pitched his fifth no-hitter, breaking

crackle as he aged. He notchec
hitter at age 43. A year later, M
his back killing him, his left he
every time he put weight c
nonetheless retired 26 batte
yielding a hit. A thin smile purs
the next hitter approached the
Toronto Blue Jays. It was Robe
son of Sandy Alomar, a Ryan
the 1970s. "He played catch v
my brother when we were
Roberto remembered fondly. Moments later, the old man str
kid with a 95-mph fastball and had his seventh no-hitter —
than anyone else. In those seven games, batters went 0-for-19

DON LARSEN

PITCHES THE ONLY WORLD SERIES PERFECT GAME

There were 152,666 Major League Baseball games played in the 20th century, which means that 305,332 pitchers had an opportunity to achieve a perfect game — retiring all batters without any reaching base. Only 14 did. On average, it happened once every seven years, once every 10,900 games. The list of 14 includes five Hall of Fame pitchers — but it does not include the likes of Christy Mathewson, Lefty Grove, Grover Cleveland Alexander, Warren Spahn, Walter Johnson, Roger Clemens, Steve Carlton, Whitey Ford, Nolan Ryan, Bob Gibson, Tom Seaver. Those immortals on their greatest day were not as good as Don Larsen was on his greatest day. Even among the perfect-game pitchers, Larsen stands alone, for he was the only one to achieve the feat on baseball's biggest stage, the World Series. No one else, in fact, has even pitched a no-hitter in the World Series or in the postseason series that now precede it.

Larsen pitched for 14 seasons in the major leagues and ended his career with a modest 81-91 record. One year he went 3-21. For every nine innings he pitched, he gave up an average of eight hits and four walks. Larsen clearly had talent, but he also had a reputation for losing focus and purpose on the mound. Teammates called him "Gooneybird." He was a voracious reader of comic books and had an affinity for the nightlife. After Larsen wrecked his car during the wee hours of the morning one spring, Yankees manager Casey Stengel deadpanned, "He must've been going to the post office to mail a letter."

If a New York Yankees pitcher were destined to rise above the human condition in 1956 and achieve perfection, it surely would have been 19-game winner Whitey Ford, 18-game winner Johnny Kucks or 16-game winner Tom Sturdivant. Larsen went 11-5 — it would prove to be the best

For two hours and six minutes, the 27-year-old Larsen practiced the craft of pitching
BETTER THAN ALMOST ANYONE WHO EVER LIVED.

PERFECT GAMES IN THE 20th CENTURY

PITCHER	DATE OF GAME	OPPONENT/SCORE
* CY YOUNG BOSTON RED SOX	MAY 5, 1904	PHILADELPHIA ATHLETICS, 3-0
* ADDIE JOSS CLEVELAND INDIANS	OCTOBER 2, 1908	CHICAGO WHITE SOX, 1-0
CHARLIE ROBERTSON CHICAGO WHITE SOX	APRIL 30, 1922	DETROIT TIGERS, 2-0
DON LARSEN NEW YORK YANKEES	OCTOBER 8, 1956	BROOKLYN DODGERS, 2-0
* JIM BUNNING PHILADELPHIA PHILLIES	JUNE 21, 1964	NEW YORK METS, 6-0
* SANDY KOUFAX LOS ANGELES DODGERS	SEPTEMBER 9, 1965	CHICAGO CUBS, 1-0
* CATFISH HUNTER OAKLAND ATHLETICS	MAY 8, 1968	MINNESOTA TWINS, 4-0
LEN BARKER CLEVELAND INDIANS	MAY 15, 1981	TORONTO BLUE JAYS, 3-0
MIKE WITT CALIFORNIA ANGELS	SEPTEMBER 30, 1984	TEXAS RANGERS, 1-0
TOM BROWNING CINCINNATI REDS	SEPTEMBER 16, 1988	LOS ANGELES DODGERS, 1-0
DENNIS MARTINEZ MONTREAL EXPOS	JULY 28, 1991	LOS ANGELES DODGERS, 2-0
KENNY ROGERS TEXAS RANGERS	JULY 28, 1994	CALIFORNIA ANGELS, 4-0
DAVID WELLS NEW YORK YANKEES	MAY 17, 1998	MINNESOTA TWINS, 4-0
DAVE CONE NEW YORK YANKEES	JULY 18, 1999	MONTREAL EXPOS, 6-0
* HALL OF FAME		

THE VICTIMS

Here is the Brooklyn Dodgers lineup that Don Larsen faced on October 8, 1956,
and their statistics for the regular season.
REESE, SNIDER, ROBINSON AND CAMPANELLA ARE IN THE HALL OF FAME.

PLAYER	POS	G	HR	RBI	SB	BA	PLAYER	POS	G	HR	RBI	SB	BA
JUNIOR GILLIAM	2B	153	6	43	21	.300	SANDY AMOROS	LF	114	16	58	3	.260
PEE WEE REESE	SS	147	9	46	13	.257	CARL FURILLO	RF	149	21	83	1	.289
DUKE SNIDER	CF	151	43	101	3	.292	ROY CAMPANELLA	C	124	20	73	1	.219
JACKIE ROBINSON	3B	117	10	43	12	.275	SAL MAGLIE	P	28	0	2	0	.129
GIL HODGES	1B	153	32	87	3	.265	DALE MITCHELL	PH	57	0	7	0	.204

No one, least of all Larsen, knows
WHAT CAME OVER HIM THAT DAY.

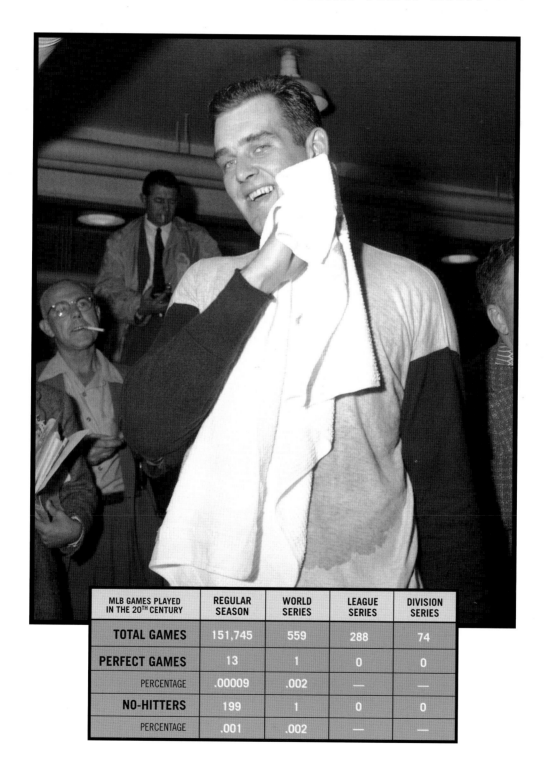

MLB GAMES PLAYED IN THE 20TH CENTURY	REGULAR SEASON	WORLD SERIES	LEAGUE SERIES	DIVISION SERIES
TOTAL GAMES	151,745	559	288	74
PERFECT GAMES	13	1	0	0
PERCENTAGE	.00009	.002	—	—
NO-HITTERS	199	1	0	0
PERCENTAGE	.001	.002	—	—

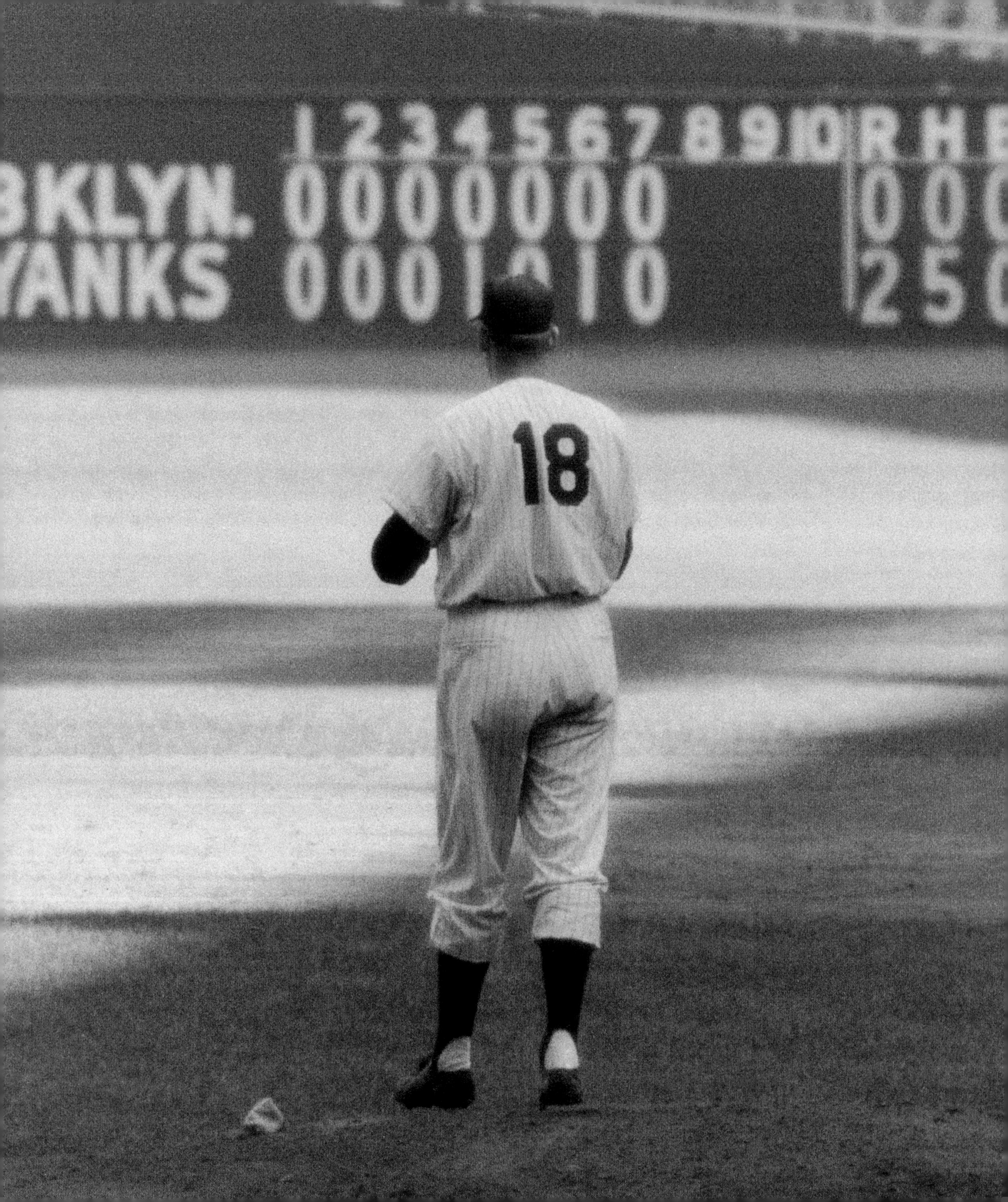
1 2 3 4 5 6 7 8 9 10 R H E
BKLYN. 0 0 0 0 0 0 0
YANKS
18

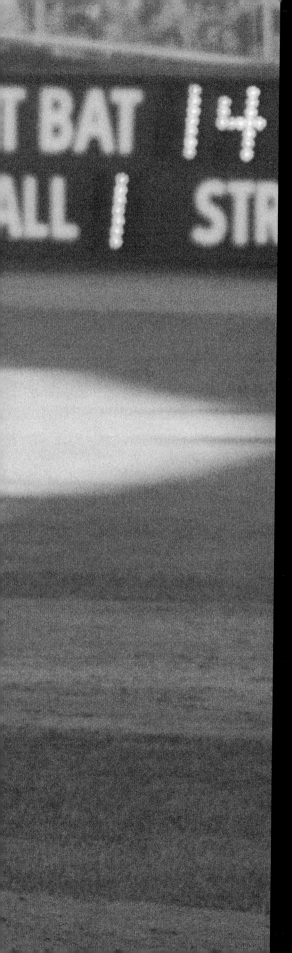

season of his career — but he didn't make it through the second inning against the Brooklyn Dodgers in the second game of the World Series. Stengel sent out Larsen again for the fifth game on the afternoon of October 8.

No one, least of all Larsen, knows what came over him that day. He worked from a stretch position because he had lost confidence in his ability to pitch from a traditional windup. Inning by inning, batter by batter, pitching with skill, guile and poise he had never known, Larsen sat down a lineup that included Jackie Robinson, Pee Wee Reese, Duke Snider and Roy Campanella, all Hall of Fame–bound players. He went to a ball-three count only once, and the Yankees made only three plays behind him that were considered above the norm.

For two hours and six minutes, the 27-year-old Larsen practiced the craft of pitching better than almost anyone who ever lived. When it was over, the Yankees had a 2-0 victory and the tall, broad-shouldered Larsen had Yogi Berra in his arms, a celebratory embrace that is one of the most lasting sports images of the era. The next year, the perfect pitcher became Don Larsen again, a condition he could live with because he had proved there is a cure: Anything is possible.

PERFECT GAME PITCHERS AND THEIR CAREERS

(LISTED BY NUMBER OF VICTORIES)

PLAYER	YRs	W	L	ERA	GS	ShO
CY YOUNG	22	511	316	2.63	815	76
POSTSEASON		2	1	1.59	3	0
DENNIS MARTINEZ	23	245	193	3.70	562	30
POSTSEASON		2	2	3.39	7	0
CATFISH HUNTER	15	224	166	3.26	476	42
POSTSEASON		9	6	3.26	19	1
JIM BUNNING	17	224	184	3.27	519	40
DAVID CONE	16	193	123	3.44	415	22
POSTSEASON		8	3	3.80	18	0
DAVID WELLS	15	166	114	4.08	325	10
POSTSEASON		8	1	2.74	10	0
SANDY KOUFAX	12	165	87	2.76	314	40
POSTSEASON		4	3	0.95	7	2
ADDIE JOSS	9	160	97	1.88	260	46
KENNY ROGERS	13	132	98	4.23	271	6
POSTSEASON		0	3	9.47	5	0
TOM BROWNING	12	123	90	3.94	300	12
POSTSEASON		2	1	3.71	3	0
MIKE WITT	12	117	116	3.83	299	11
POSTSEASON		1	0	3.05	2	0
DON LARSEN	14	81	91	3.78	171	11
POSTSEASON		4	2	2.75	6	1
LEN BARKER	11	74	76	4.35	194	6
CHARLIE ROBERTSON	8	49	80	4.44	142	6

ROGERS AND WELLS ARE ACTIVE PLAYERS; THEIR TOTALS ARE THROUGH THE 2001 SEASON

(1975)
CARLTON FISK
ENDS GAME 6 OF THE WORLD SERIES WITH A HOME RUN

The image remains vivid: Carlton Fisk dropping his bat, hopping sideways a few steps toward first base, eyes riveted on the baseball he has driven high and long through the damp air to left field, frantically waving his extended arms from left to right. Most of those in Fenway Park for the sixth game of the 1975 World Series did not witness Fisk's valiant effort to will the ball fair; like him, they were tracking the flight of the ball. Sometimes it is better not to be there. Those watching on television had the eyes of NBC's camera inside the left-field wall, the Green Monster. Legendary director Harry Coyle kept that camera hot, choosing human emotion instead of a white blur in the sky. The ball struck the mesh attached to the right side of the left-field foul pole — a home run for Fisk and a 7-6 victory in 12 innings for the Boston Red Sox over the Cincinnati Reds.

Television has never been a more powerful medium for Major League Baseball than it was that night, er, morning — Fisk connected at 34 minutes past midnight on October 22. *TV Guide* selected the Fisk footage as the No. 1 video sports moment of the 20th century. It brought a stunning and fitful end to a game that had been gripped throughout by drama and emotion. Some believe it was the greatest baseball game ever played, among them Pete Rose, who declared as much to Fisk, the Red Sox catcher, as he prepared to bat in the 11th inning. Rose can speak authoritatively on that matter; no one has played in more Major League Baseball games than he has.

Pop sociologists claim that Game 6 of the 1975 World Series saved baseball; at the least, it revived the game in the conscience of the American public. The late 1960s and early 1970s was an era of anger in the United

Carlton Fisk, best remembered for his 12th-inning home run in Game 6 of the 1975 World Series, had a long and illustrious career. He proved to be one of Major League Baseball's most enduring performers, playing into his 45th year. Fisk is the all-time best power hitter among the *fortysomething* set.

MOST HOME RUNS PAST AGE 40

CARLTON FISK	72	TED WILLIAMS	44
DARRELL EVANS	60	HANK AARON	42
DAVE WINFIELD	59	GRAIG NETTLES	40
CARL YASTRZEMSKI	49	HANK SAUER	39
STAN MUSIAL	46	HAROLD BAINES	36

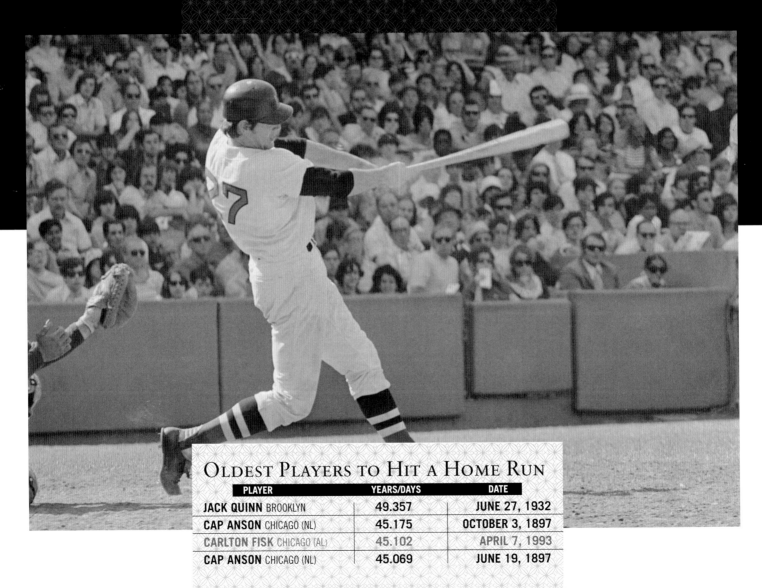

OLDEST PLAYERS TO HIT A HOME RUN

PLAYER	YEARS/DAYS	DATE
JACK QUINN BROOKLYN	49.357	JUNE 27, 1932
CAP ANSON CHICAGO (NL)	45.175	OCTOBER 3, 1897
CARLTON FISK CHICAGO (AL)	45.102	APRIL 7, 1993
CAP ANSON CHICAGO (NL)	45.069	JUNE 19, 1897

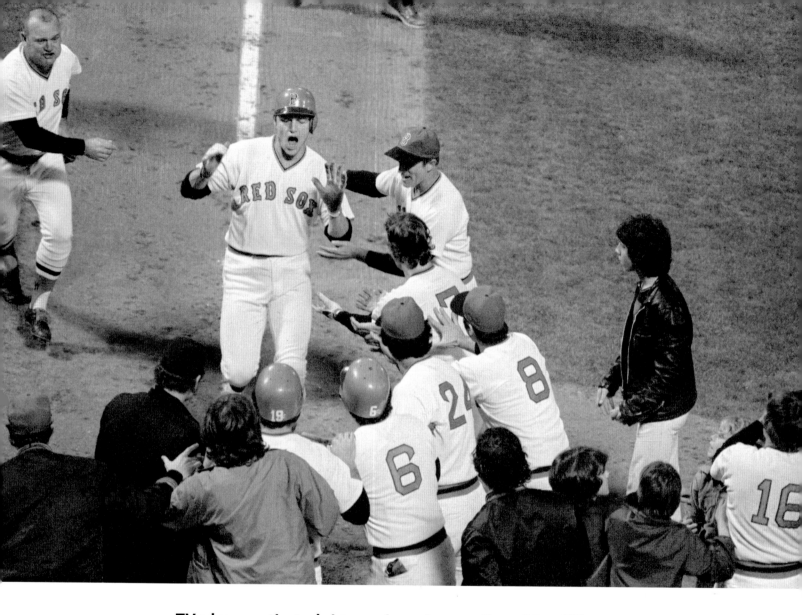

TV viewers that night numbered more than 60 million.
THEY WATCHED FISK, BY WILL AND WANT, DIRECT HIS FLY BALL FAIR.

States. Social unrest prevailed. War raged in Vietnam. Nixon resigned in disgrace. African-Americans demanded equal rights. Disillusioned youth revolted. Cities burned. America simmered, and for entertainment the pounding violence of football provided a more compelling outlet than the leisurely pace of baseball. *Monday Night Football* was a cultural phenomenon. Baseball, trying to keep up, replaced treasured parks and green grass with generic circular concrete stadiums and AstroTurf, homogenizing in an age of individuality.

Then America tuned in to the 1975 World Series and turned on to baseball again. The Red Sox and the Reds engaged in a spirited match over 12 days that celebrated all the drama, excitement and passion the game played at its highest level can provide. By Game 6, fans were coming back in droves — TV viewers that night numbered more than 60 million. They watched Fisk, by will and want, direct his fly ball fair. A day later they watched the Red Sox return to their rightful place in the universe — Boston lost Game 7, perpetuating the Series failures that began after the team's last win in 1918.

Maris posed with Sal Durante, the fan who caught the 61st home run ball.

(1961)
ROGER MARIS
BREAKS BABE RUTH'S SEASON HOME RUN RECORD

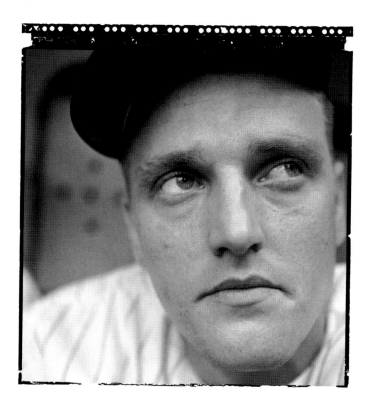

Roger Maris arrived in Keokuk, Iowa, for the summer of 1954, climbing the minor-league ladder. Keokuk manager Jo-Jo White watched the strapping, young left-handed batter spraying the ball to all fields and quickly interrupted. "Look, boy," White bellowed, "you're not a singles hitter. You're big and you've got power. Pull that ball to right field and see what happens." White's sage advice would carry Maris to unprecedented heights in the game — and also bring him unwarranted pain and revilement.

No other ballplayer has ever pulled the ball quite as effectively and efficiently as Maris did during the 1961 season. He had joined the New York Yankees the previous season and proved to be a fine player. Maris played with a burning intensity, was a superb rightfielder with an exceptionally strong arm, and rarely ever made a mistake while running the bases. But his greatest attribute was a quick, pull swing with a slight uppercut that was ideal for Yankee Stadium, where the right-field bleachers sat little more than 300 feet from home plate. Few of Maris's home runs traveled as far as 400 feet; most dropped into the early rows of seats in the lower deck of the stadium.

The 1961 season promised to be an offensive awakening, especially in the American League, which had new teams in Los Angeles and

"I NEVER WANTED ALL THIS HOOPLA.
All I wanted is to be a good ballplayer and hit 25 or 30 homers, drive in 100 runs,
hit .280, and help my club win pennants.
I JUST WANTED TO BE ONE OF THE GUYS,
an average player having a good season."
— ROGER MARIS

Maris followed the flight of his historic home run.

Washington, D.C., and with them at least 20 pitchers who otherwise wouldn't be considered major-league quality. In addition, the schedule had been extended from 154 to 162 games. No one, though, expected an assault on the most hallowed record in sport: Babe Ruth's 60 home runs in a season. Maris and his more celebrated teammate, Mickey Mantle, took up the chase, and both were still on pace for the record in late August.

Mantle dropped out in September because of a hip injury, leaving Maris to go it alone. The public and press had been chilly to Maris' mounting home run total, all along favoring Mantle, a larger-than-life and charismatic player in the great tradition of Yankees legends. Once Maris became the only threat to Ruth, the environment about him was charged with hostility and even hatred. The relentless pressure caused his hair to fall out in clumps and turned his personality sour. The career .260 hitter found solace only in the batter's box, where he could slip into the one-on-one battle with a pitcher and erase everything else from his consciousness.

The homers kept coming. On October 1, the final day of the season, the battle-weary Maris connected with a 2-and-0 fastball from Tracy Stallard of the Boston Red Sox and dropped it some 340 feet into the right-field seats at Yankee's Stadium for his 61st homer. The crowd that day was a mere 23,154, a third of the stadium's capacity. Baseball almost seemed ashamed of Maris's feat. Commissioner Ford Frick had decreed that Maris would have to set the record in 154 games for it to be official, and Yankees management declined to promote Maris's chase — all in deference to the godlike Ruth.

Yet Maris held the record longer than Ruth. The Babe's achievement held up for 34 years. It was 37 years later, in 1998, that both Mark McGwire and Sammy Sosa surpassed Maris's record.

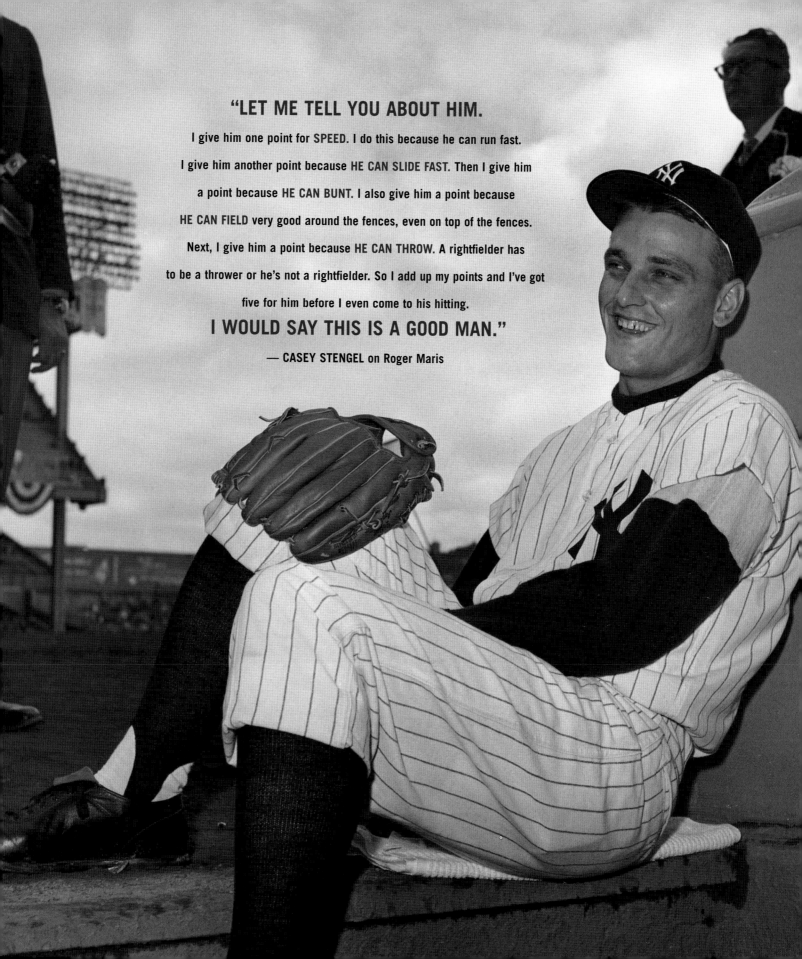

"LET ME TELL YOU ABOUT HIM.

I give him one point for SPEED. I do this because he can run fast.

I give him another point because HE CAN SLIDE FAST. Then I give him

a point because HE CAN BUNT. I also give him a point because

HE CAN FIELD very good around the fences, even on top of the fences.

Next, I give him a point because HE CAN THROW. A rightfielder has

to be a thrower or he's not a rightfielder. So I add up my points and I've got

five for him before I even come to his hitting.

I WOULD SAY THIS IS A GOOD MAN."

— CASEY STENGEL on Roger Maris

BEST TO NEXT

Roger Maris's second-best home run total was 39. The following list shows players who had the greatest difference between their best and second-best home run seasons. Alfonso Soriano was on pace in 2002 to join the list.

PLAYER	BEST	SECOND BEST	DIFF.
BRADY ANDERSON	50 (1996)	24 (1999)	26
LUIS GONZALEZ	57 (2001)	31 (2000)	26
RICHARD HIDALGO	44 (2000)	19 (2001)	25
DAVEY JOHNSON	43 (1973)	18 (1971)	25
BARRY BONDS	73 (2001)	49 (2000)	24
ROGER MARIS	61 (1961)	39 (1960)	22
JOE CHARBONEAU	23 (1980)	4 (1981)	19
KEN HUNT	25 (1961)	6 (1963)	19

PLAYER	BEST	SECOND BEST	DIFF.
TERRY STEINBACH	35 (1996)	16 (1987)	19
WILLARD MARSHALL	36 (1947)	17 (1953)	19
BUZZ ARLETT	18 (1931)	—	18
BOB CERV	38 (1958)	20 (1959)	18
JIM BAXES	17 (1959)	—	17
JAY BELL	38 (1999)	21 (1997)	17
ANDRE DAWSON	49 (1987)	32 (1983)	17
HACK WILSON	56 (1930)	39 (1929)	17

(1951)

BOBBY THOMSON

CONNECTS FOR THE "SHOT HEARD 'ROUND THE WORLD"

The day of reckoning dawned dark and foreboding. Summer was gone, yet there still was not a National League champion, and rain threatened to further prey on two sets of fans long since rendered emotionally raw and fatigued.

THE BROOKLYN DODGERS AND THE NEW YORK GIANTS OF THE 1940s AND 1950s ENGAGED IN THE FIERCEST RIVALRY IN SPORTS HISTORY,

and a defining moment was upon them and their fans. They were tied for first place after a 154-game season, and again after the first two games of a best-of-three playoff series. They had played each other 24 times, and finally there was no tomorrow — unless it rained — for two municipalities that were separated only by a bridge but might as well have been on different sides of the ocean.

THOMSON'S NEW YORK SEASONS

	G	HR	RBI	BA
1946	18	2	9	.315
1947	138	29	85	.283
1948	138	16	63	.248
1949	156	27	109	.309
1950	149	25	85	.252
1951	148	32	101	.293
1952	153	24	108	.270
1953	154	26	106	.288
1957	81	8	38	.302

Brooklyn vs. New York was more than a rivalry; it was a way of life. Brooklyn was a town; Manhattan was a city. Brooklyn was blue collar and neighborhoods, home to cab drivers, plumbers, civil servants, bowlers; Manhattan was white collar and high society, home to stockbrokers, investment bankers, the movers and shakers of the world. You had to live it to understand it, and some lived it to the end, including the native Brooklynite seated in the electric chair at the Massachusetts State Prison in April 1941 who asked the warden, "Did da Bums win against the Giants today?" The ties were just as deep for the players. Witness pitcher Freddie Fitzsimmons, a grown man who bawled like a baby when the cab carrying him left Manhattan soil and crossed the Brooklyn Bridge after the Giants traded him to the Dodgers in 1937.

The skies held on October 3, 1951, but it was dark enough by mid-afternoon that the lights were on at the Polo Grounds, home of the Giants. At game time, perhaps only 34,000 of the 60,000 seats were occupied. The weather — or maybe it was the threat of impending heartbreak

Thomson dashes for the clubhouse after his famous home run, leaving ecstatic Giants fans to celebrate without him.

IT AIN'T OVER 'TIL IT'S OVER

The 1951 New York Giants staged one of the great comebacks in Major League Baseball history just to put Bobby Thomson in position to hit the "Shot Heard 'Round the World." Here is a list of the 17 teams that have made up deficits of 10 games or more in the standings and won the pennant or a division title.

TEAM	GAMES BEHIND	ON	W-L	FINAL W-L	GAMES AHEAD	TEAM	GAMES BEHIND	ON	W-L	FINAL W-L	GAMES AHEAD
1914 BOSTON BRAVES	15.0	JULY 5	26-40	94-59	10.5	1987 * DETROIT TIGERS	11.0	MAY 5	9-16	98-64	2.0
1978 * NEW YORK YANKEES	14.0	JULY 19	48-42	100-63	1.0	1935 CHICAGO CUBS	10.5	JULY 5	38-32	100-54	4.0
1951 NEW YORK GIANTS	13.5	AUGUST 11	59-51	98-59	1.0	1936 NEW YORK GIANTS	10.5	JULY 16	42-41	92-62	5.0
1995 * SEATTLE MARINERS	13.0	AUGUST 2	43-46	79-66	1.0	1979 * CINCINNATI REDS	10.5	JULY 4	41-41	90-71	1.5
1973 * NEW YORK METS	12.5	JULY 8	34-46	82-79	1.5	1942 ST. LOUIS CARDINALS	10.0	AUGUST 5	63-39	106-48	2.0
1911 PHILADELPHIA ATHLETICS	12.0	MAY 19	13-15	101-50	13.5	1988 * BOSTON RED SOX	10.0	JUNE 13	28-30	89-73	1.0
1930 ST. LOUIS CARDINALS	12.0	AUGUST 8	53-52	92-62	2.0	1989 * TORONTO BLUE JAYS	10.0	JULY 5	38-45	89-73	2.0
1964 ST. LOUIS CARDINALS	11.0	AUGUST 23	65-58	93-69	1.0	1993 * ATLANTA BRAVES	10.0	JULY 22	55-42	104-58	1.0
1973 * CINCINNATI REDS	11.0	JUNE 30	39-37	99-63	3.5						

* DIVISION CHAMPIONSHIP   THROUGH 2001 SEASON

Thomson shared an embrace with Giants owner Horace Stoneham and manager Leo Durocher after the game.

witnessed firsthand — kept most fans away, taking their medicine by radio. Millions listened to Russ Hodges and Red Barber on the local airwaves, while Gordon McClendon called the action for the rest of America on the Liberty Radio Network.

Leo Durocher's plucky Giants had pulled off one of the greatest comebacks in baseball history, winning 37 of the final 44 games, 16 consecutive at one juncture, and making up 13½ games on the Dodgers in seven weeks. But they needed another comeback to complete this miracle, and a tall, handsome lad from Staten Island stepped up to the plate. Bobby Thomson drove a fastball from Ralph Branca through the dreary muck, and it

climbed just over the 17-foot high left-field wall at the 315-foot marker, nestling into the cheap seats. The three-run homer in the bottom of the ninth inning, the "Shot Heard 'Round the World," as it came to be known, gave the Giants a 5-4 victory and the pennant. Hodges screamed on the radio, eight times without stopping, "The Giants win the pennant!" The rookie in the on-deck circle, Willie Mays, quit trembling. Manhattan erupted in a wild frenzy; Brooklyn suffocated in quiet despair. The man of the hour — for some, the man of the ages — circled the bases, and for an instant Thomson's joy was tempered. He remembered that his dead father had been a Dodgers fan.

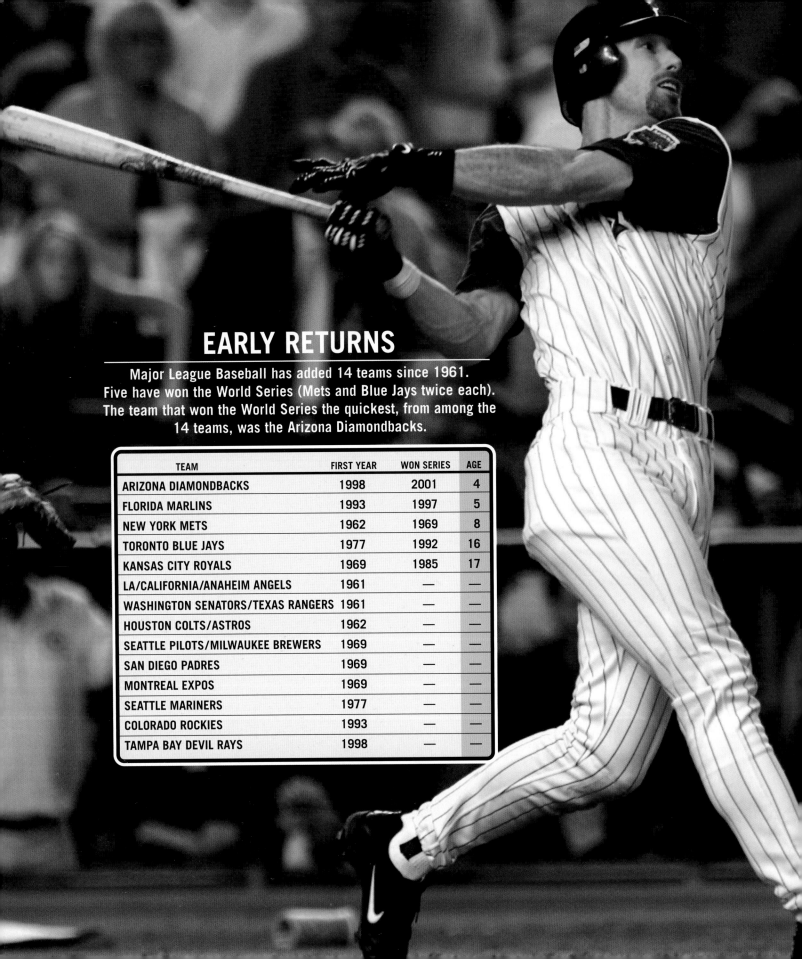

EARLY RETURNS

Major League Baseball has added 14 teams since 1961.
Five have won the World Series (Mets and Blue Jays twice each).
The team that won the World Series the quickest, from among the
14 teams, was the Arizona Diamondbacks.

TEAM	FIRST YEAR	WON SERIES	AGE
ARIZONA DIAMONDBACKS	1998	2001	4
FLORIDA MARLINS	1993	1997	5
NEW YORK METS	1962	1969	8
TORONTO BLUE JAYS	1977	1992	16
KANSAS CITY ROYALS	1969	1985	17
LA/CALIFORNIA/ANAHEIM ANGELS	1961	—	—
WASHINGTON SENATORS/TEXAS RANGERS	1961	—	—
HOUSTON COLTS/ASTROS	1962	—	—
SEATTLE PILOTS/MILWAUKEE BREWERS	1969	—	—
SAN DIEGO PADRES	1969	—	—
MONTREAL EXPOS	1969	—	—
SEATTLE MARINERS	1977	—	—
COLORADO ROCKIES	1993	—	—
TAMPA BAY DEVIL RAYS	1998	—	—

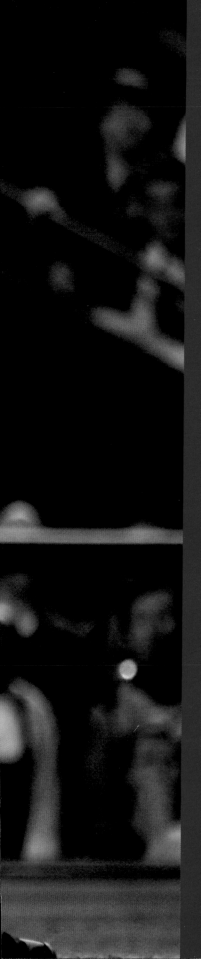

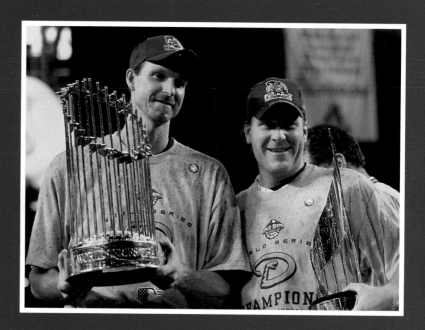

(2001)
ARIZONA DIAMONDBACKS
WIN GAME 7 OF THE WORLD SERIES IN THE BOTTOM OF THE NINTH INNING

Bonds splashed 73 home runs, more than Ruth, Maris, McGwire or anyone else in history. The Mariners, soldiering on without Junior, Big Unit or A-Rod, won 116 games, as many as any other team in history. Could the plots in Major League Baseball get any richer in 2001? Well, catch your breath, and take in the World Series — it proved to be among the most compelling of all time.

The Yankees, aristocrats of all sport, with 26 World Championships in their bag, were back for a fourth straight trophy, a fifth in six years. On the National League side stood the Arizona Diamondbacks, four years in the root, not a shred of tradition, a team of transients. They lacked in pedigree, but they had Randy Johnson and Curt Schilling, a feared lefty and a precision righty, a 1-2 pitching combination as awesome as any the game had ever seen.

That pair claimed the first two games, and by Game 4 it was apparent that the desert upstarts represented a real threat to the establishment. The Diamondbacks had a 3-1 lead with two outs in the bottom of the ninth inning and were about to take a 3-1 Series edge. Byung-Hyun Kim, a 22-year-old sidewinder from Korea, tried to sneak a belt-high fastball past Tino Martinez, but Martinez sent the ball into the night and over the center-field fence, tying the score. Fifteen minutes later, Kim failed again, delivering a 10th-inning gopher ball to Derek Jeter that left the Yankees improbable 4-3 winners. As though they were Broadway thespians, the Yankees staged a repeat performance less than 24 hours later. Kim again was on the hook for the Diamondbacks with two outs in the ninth inning, charged with holding a 2-1 lead. Again he caved, his offering dropped over the left-field fence by Scott Brosius. An hour later, Alfonso Soriano drove home the decisive run with a single. On consecutive nights, the Yankees had overcome two-run deficits in the ninth inning and won — an achievement equaled only four previous times in 96 World Series.

WORLD SERIES THREE-GAME WINNERS

YEAR	PLAYER	OPPONENT
2001	RANDY JOHNSON ARIZONA DIAMONDBACKS	NEW YORK YANKEES
1968	MICKEY LOLICH DETROIT TIGERS	ST. LOUIS CARDINALS
1967	BOB GIBSON ST. LOUIS CARDINALS	BOSTON RED SOX
1957	LEW BURDETTE MILWAUKEE BRAVES	NEW YORK YANKEES
1946	HERRY BRECHEEN ST. LOUIS CARDINALS	BOSTON RED SOX
1920	STAN COVELESKI CLEVELAND INDIANS	BROOKLYN DODGERS
1917	URBAN FABER CHICAGO WHITE SOX	NEW YORK GIANTS
1912	SMOKEY JOE WOOD BOSTON RED SOX	NEW YORK GIANTS
1910	JOHN COOMBS PHILADELPHIA ATHLETICS	CHICAGO CUBS
1909	BABE ADAMS PITTSBURGH PIRATES	DETROIT TIGERS
1905	CHRISTY MATHEWSON NEW YORK GIANTS	PHILADELPHIA ATHLETICS
1903	WILLIAM DINEEN BOSTON RED SOX	PITTSBURGH PIRATES
1903	* DEACON PHILLIPPE PITTSBURGH PIRATES	BOSTON RED SOX

ONLY THREE-GAME WINNER WHOSE TEAM DID NOT WIN THE WORLD SERIES

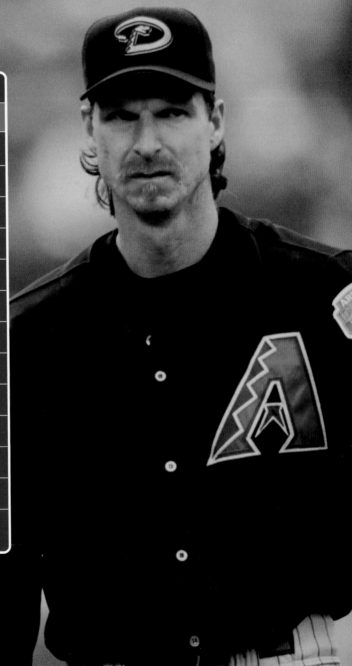

North America was transfixed on the Series by this point. Game 6 in Phoenix, Johnson in command, was a 15-2 blowout for the Diamondbacks. Now for destiny, Schilling vs. Clemens, no tomorrow. Both did their damnedest, along with Johnson, who claimed the final four Yankees outs and became the first in 33 years to win three games in a Series. It went to the bottom of the ninth with the Diamondbacks on the

November since 1998, on the mound The rest is baseball lore. Two hits, an error, and Luis Gonzalez, a 57-home man during the season, summoning all of his might and plunking a weak single just beyond the infield that brough home the winning run, 3-2. A bleeder had done in the three-time champs and brought the first World Championship trophy of any kind to the 48th state. Memorable moment

(1954)
WILLIE MAYS
MAKES A SENSATIONAL CATCH IN THE WORLD SERIES

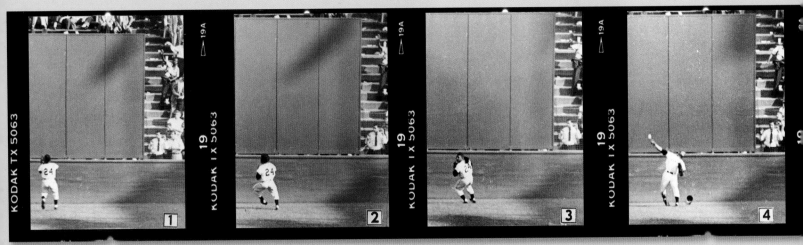

A frame-by-frame look at "The Catch."

F ew, if any, have ever played baseball as instinctively as Willie Mays did. Whether he was batting, running the bases or patrolling center field, his capacity for the game and lightning-quick intuition seemed to keep him a half-stroke ahead of everyone else on the diamond. Mays once chased down a long fly and without hesitation threw the ball to second baseman Tito Fuentes and directed him to touch the bag. Fuentes did as he was told, and Hank Aaron was called out. Aaron had been on first base and advanced past second base on the fly ball, only to retreat to first after the catch. How did Mays, with his back to the infield, possibly know Aaron had not touched second? Willie just shrugged and said, "I know the way he runs."

Mays indeed was the artist, and his canvas was center field in the Polo Grounds, the greatest expanse in Major League Baseball in the 1950s. The Giants's home field was shaped like a horseshoe, which made for cramped quarters in right and left fields but a vast sea of green in between. It took a tremendous drive to reach the fence in the alleys, and a gargantuan blast would merely challenge the center-field wall, 483 feet from home plate. In 49 years' worth of games at the Polo Grounds, including double duty when the New York Yankees and the Negro League teams also used the place, only Luke Easter, Joe Adcock, Lou Brock and Hank Aaron put enough bat on ball to reach the center-field bleachers. Someone had to chase down everything else in those wide-open spaces, and Mays did it better than anyone before or after him.

It was an age when television sets were multiplying as fast as rabbits. By 1954, half of the 25 million households in the United States owned a TV, and many were tuned in when the World Series opened that year, pitting the Cleveland Indians, fresh off a record-setting 111-victory season, against the

★★★

Willie Mays had plenty of room to roam in center field at the
Polo Grounds — the fence was 483 feet from home plate.
If Mark McGwire and Sammy Sosa in 1998 and Barry Bonds
in 2001 had to hit the ball that far for a home run,
THE THREE WOULD HAVE HIT NINE HOME RUNS ALTOGETHER.

McGWIRE'S LONGEST HOME RUNS IN 1998

NO.	FEET	CITY	PARK	PITCHER, TEAM
16	545	ST. LOUIS	BUSCH STADIUM	LIVAN HERNANDEZ, FLORIDA
14	527	ST. LOUIS	BUSCH STADIUM	PAUL WAGNER, MILWAUKEE
41	511	ST. LOUIS	BUSCH STADIUM	BRIAN BOHANON, LOS ANGELES
54	509	ST. LOUIS	BUSCH STADIUM	JUSTIN SPEIER, FLORIDA
55	501	ST. LOUIS	BUSCH STADIUM	DENNIS MARTINEZ, ATLANTA
58	497	MIAMI	PRO PLAYER PARK	BRIAN EDMONDSON, FLORIDA
38	485	ST. LOUIS	BUSCH STADIUM	BILLY WAGNER, HOUSTON
17	478	ST. LOUIS	BUSCH STADIUM	JESUS SANCHEZ, FLORIDA

SOSA'S LONGEST HOME RUNS IN 1998

NO.	FEET	CITY	PARK	PITCHER, TEAM
29	500	CHICAGO	WRIGLEY FIELD	TOBY BORLAND, PHILADELPHIA
54	482	DENVER	COORS FIELD	DARRYL KILE, COLORADO
46	480	SAN FRANCISCO	3COM PARK	CHRIS BROCK, SAN FRANCISCO
61	480	CHICAGO	WRIGLEY FIELD	BRONSWELL PATRICK, MILWAUKEE
62	480	CHICAGO	WRIGLEY FIELD	ERIC PLUNK, MILWAUKEE

BONDS'S LONGEST HOME RUNS IN 2001

NO.	FEET	CITY	PARK	PITCHER, TEAM
61	488	DENVER	COORS FIELD	SCOTT ELARTON, COLORADO
70	480	HOUSTON	ENRON FIELD	WILFREDO RODRIGUEZ, HOUSTON
32	450	SAN FRANCISCO	PACIFIC BELL PARK	BRIAN LAWRENCE, SAN DIEGO

Giants. The first game was at the Polo Grounds, and what transpired in the eighth inning that day provided the first evidence of how powerful a force TV would prove to be in the sports world.

With runners on first and second, no outs and the score tied 2-2, Vic Wertz connected dead-on with a fastball and sent it on a screaming rise toward the outer reaches of center field. The intuitive Mays turned and was on his horse before the ball left the bat, sprinting 50 to 60 yards and catching the ball on the dead run over his left shoulder near the warning track. That was just the half of it. All in the same motion of the catch, Mays spun violently on his left leg and delivered the ball like a laser beam

to the cutoff man. The runner on second managed to get to third, but the runner on first stayed put.

The crowd, some 55,000, couldn't believe what they had just seen. A few years earlier those patrons would have been the only witnesses. But all over America, baseball fans carried on about Mays's incredible catch and throw, a performance that had played out grainy but surreal on their black-and-white screens at home. There have been many astounding defensive plays in baseball history, but Mays's remains the most famous, growing in legend over the years, probably because it was the first one that TV enabled to transcend the ballpark.

(2001)
BARRY BONDS
PUSHES THE HOME RUN
RECORD TO 73

Barry Bonds was the most brilliant ballplayer of his generation, unmatched for his ability as a hitter, fielder and baserunner. He had MVP awards, Gold Gloves, more 30–home run/30–stolen base seasons than anyone else in history. His legacy was numbing consistency, marvelous performance year in and year out. The only thing missing was the signature season that would truly put him on the same playing field as the gods of the game. That finally would come in his 36th year, his 16th in the major leagues, his ninth with the San Francisco Giants.

Bonds hit a home run on Opening Day of the 2001 season, leaving him five short of 500, a significant achievement in any baseball lifetime. In this case, reaching 500 was a short-lived celebration, for Bonds was embarking on what some baseball historians consider to be the greatest season ever achieved by a ballplayer.

EVOLUTION OF THE HOME RUN RECORD		
GEORGE HALL PHILADELPHIA PHILLIES	1876	5
CHARLEY JONES BOSTON BRAVES	1879	9
HARRY STOVEY PHILADELPHIA PHILLIES	1883	14
NED WILLIAMSON CHICAGO CUBS	1884	27
BABE RUTH BOSTON RED SOX	1919	29
BABE RUTH NEW YORK YANKEES	1920	54
BABE RUTH NEW YORK YANKEES	1921	59
BABE RUTH NEW YORK YANKEES	1927	60
ROGER MARIS NEW YORK YANKEES	1961	61
MARK McGWIRE ST. LOUIS CARDINALS	1998	70
BARRY BONDS SAN FRANCISCO GIANTS	2001	73

Bonds hit 11 home runs in April, 17 in May, and 11 in June; a record 39 before the All-Star Game. He hit just six homers in July — when he marked his 37th birthday — but with 12 in both August and September, Bonds entered October with 69, one home run short of Mark McGwire's record set three years earlier.

Bonds tied McGwire's mark with a 450-foot blast in Houston on October 4. A day later at home, Bonds twice connected for home runs off

Chan Ho Park of the Los Angeles Dodgers. Bonds hit his 73rd homer on the final day of the season. The home run total was only a part of his remarkable season. His slugging percentage of .863 broke Babe Ruth's record of .847 that had stood since 1920. He drew a record 177 walks, reached base almost 52 percent of the time and batted .328.

Still, the sporting public wasn't nearly as transfixed on Bonds's pursuit of the home-run record as it had been when both McGwire and Sos-

73 HOME RUNS, INNING BY INNING

INNING	1	2	3	4	5	6	7	8	9	10	11
HOME RUNS	12	5	8	12	9	7	6	9	3	0	2

The only thing missing was the signature season
that would truly put him on the same playing field as
THE GODS OF THE GAME.
That finally would come in his 36th year, his 16th in the major leagues,
his ninth with the San Francisco Giants.

Bonds's 10-year-old daughter implored pitchers on her dad's behalf, and watercraft by the dozens patrolled McCovey Cove hoping to retrieve a Bonds splash-down.

chased the record in 1998. They went up against the ghosts of the game; only one man in 71 years —Roger Maris in 1961 — had hit more than 60 homers in a season. Another chase three years later, epic as it might have been, simply did not arouse the same level of curiosity and fervor.

Bonds also had an image problem. He long had a contentious relationship with sportswriters, who often portrayed him as rude, mean-spirited and arrogant. But those who looked closely during the 2001 season saw a softer side. During a pregame ceremony, when baseball resumed its schedule a week after the September 11 terrorist attacks on the United States, Bonds had tears in his eyes as he sang "God Bless America" and "The Star Spangled Banner." And with his every moment of glory in those waning days of the season, he unfailingly acknowledged his adoring family in the crowd. A lasting image shows Bonds's young daughters holding a sign that read, "Pitch to Our Daddy!" Enough did so that Bonds crafted a season for the ages.

(1920)

BABE RUTH
LEAVES THE RED SOX FOR THE YANKEES

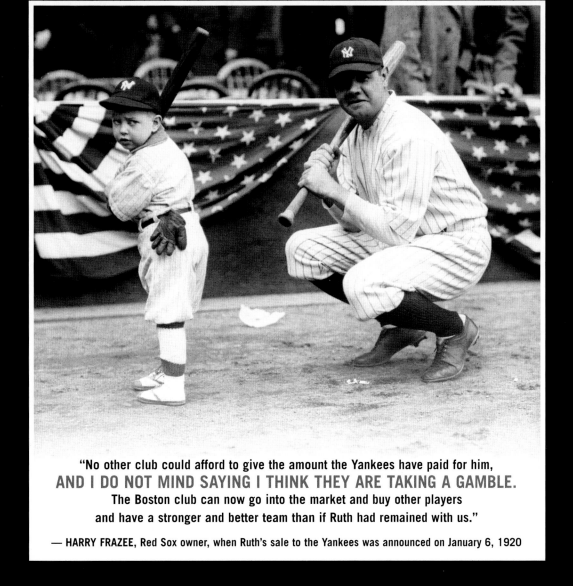

"No other club could afford to give the amount the Yankees have paid for him,
AND I DO NOT MIND SAYING I THINK THEY ARE TAKING A GAMBLE.
The Boston club can now go into the market and buy other players
and have a stronger and better team than if Ruth had remained with us."

— HARRY FRAZEE, Red Sox owner, when Ruth's sale to the Yankees was announced on January 6, 1920

Major League Baseball's integrity was seriously compromised in 1919 when some members of the Chicago White Sox conspired with gamblers and threw the World Series. The plot was unraveled in courtroom drama the following year, and disbelieving fans expressed betrayal and outrage. Some swore off the game forever; others demanded to know why they should ever again take baseball seriously. As the game's leadership speculated on how badly baseball had been damaged and whether it could thrive again, little did they know that the seeds of recovery were being sown.

On the day after Christmas in 1919, Harry Frazee unwittingly saved baseball. Frazee's intentions were not so pure when he arranged a clandestine meeting that day with the principals of the New York Yankees, whose office was within shouting distance of his own in New York's theater district. Frazee, owner of the Boston Red Sox—baseball's most successful team over the first two decades of the 20th century; winners of five of the first 15 World Series—had two problems: mounting debt and a charismatic, pigeon-toed slugger who was demanding that his salary be doubled.

Within hours Frazee had signed over the contract of Babe Ruth to the Yankees in exchange for $125,000 in cash and a $300,000 loan with Fenway Park as collateral. The cash was twice what any player had fetched previously in a sale, but it would prove to be baseball's greatest bargain. Ruth was the best left-handed pitcher of the era and so accomplished a hitter that the Red Sox had taken to using him in the outfield when he wasn't pitching. Upon arriving in New York, he succeeded in getting his salary

★★★

DEFINING DEALS

Forbes magazine rated Babe Ruth's sale to the Yankees as one of

10 "TRANSFORMING DEALS" —

transactions that helped define the companies that made them,
and in some cases transformed entire industries for better or for worse.

HERE IS THE LIST OF DEALS PUBLISHED BY *FORBES* IN MAY 2002

1919 | YANKEES PURCHASE BABE RUTH FROM RED SOX

1978 | CHRYSLER MOTORS HIRES LEE IACOCCA

1980 | MICROSOFT BUYS DISK OPERATING SYSTEM (DOS)

1988 | KOHLBERG KRAVIS ROBERTS & CO. BUYS RJR NABISCO

1992 | CBS-TV SIGNS LATE-NIGHT HOST DAVID LETTERMAN

1996 | SUN MICROSYSTEMS PURCHASES CRAY COMPUTER'S UNIX SERVER BUSINESS

1997 | SCHOLASTIC PRESS ACQUIRES HARRY POTTER RIGHTS

1998 | PE (NOW APPLERA) HIRES CRAIG VENTER

1998 | CITICORP MERGES WITH TRAVELERS TO FORM CITIGROUP

2000 | AMERICA ONLINE BUYS TIME WARNER

Babe Ruth and the Yankees owner, Colonel Jacob Ruppert, in 1930 — three World Championships into their dynasty.

doubled to $20,000, then took on larger-than-life status, booming home runs at a stunning clip and living equally large off the field. Fans forgave baseball its transgressions and returned to ballparks in droves to see the Babe, who became one of the defining symbols of The Roaring Twenties. The 1920 Yankees became the first team to surpass 1 million in home attendance, and within a few years the Yankees were the most powerful and famous team in the baseball universe, representing the most powerful and influential city in the world.

Ruth's role in luring fans back to baseball cannot be underestimated. Performing at a level above his peers', which has never been matched by any athlete in any sport — and likely never will be — he was an irresistible attraction. Consider the following: Ruth hit 54 home runs in his first season with the Yankees, more than the total of any team except his own and the Philadelphia Phillies; when he hit his 700th homer, no one else had hit even 300; and when he died in 1948, he held 56 Major League Baseball records.

As for Frazee, he remains a reviled figure in New England lore for his role in shifting the balance of baseball power from Boston to New York. The Red Sox trail the Yankees 26-0 in World Series titles since Ruth moved south. The Babe's legend was growing to mythic proportions in New York when Frazee hailed a Boston taxi one day for a ride to Fenway Park. Upon learning the identity of his passenger, the cabbie took a swing for all of New England. He dropped Frazee with one punch.

PAYBACK AVERTED

In 1925 the Yankees approached the Red Sox about an exchange of first basemen:

LOU GEHRIG FOR PHIL TODT, EVEN UP. THE RED SOX DECLINED.

Gehrig became a baseball immortal; Todt became a career .258 hitter with 57 home runs.

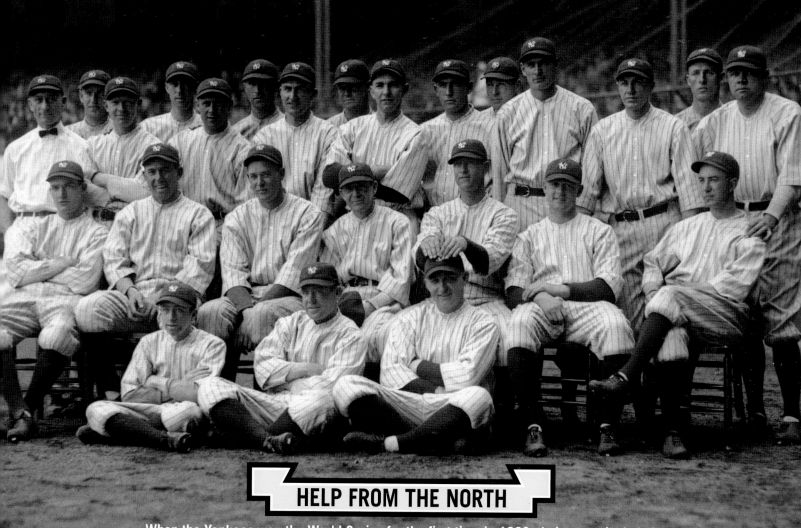

HELP FROM THE NORTH

When the Yankees won the World Series for the first time in 1923, their roster included
11 PLAYERS WHO HAD BEEN ACQUIRED FROM THE RED SOX BETWEEN 1919 AND 1922.
Here is a list of the 11 and their 1923 statistics:

BATTERS	POS.	G	HR	RBI	AVG
BABE RUTH	OF	152	41	131	.393
JOE DUGAN	3B	146	7	67	.283
EVERETT SCOTT	SS	152	6	60	.246
WALLY SCHANG	C	81	2	29	.276
MIKE MCNALLY	INF	25	0	1	.211
ELMER SMITH	OF	47	7	35	.306

PITCHERS	G	W	L	ERA
SAD SAM JONES	39	21	8	3.63
HERB PENNOCK	35	19	6	3.34
BULLET JOE BUSH	37	19	15	3.42
WAITE HOYT	37	17	9	3.01
CARL MAYS	23	5	2	6.22

(1960)

BILL MAZEROSKI
ENDS THE WORLD SERIES WITH A HOME RUN

The irony of Mazeroski is that his greatest day in baseball
WAS A RESULT OF HIS BAT, NOT HIS GLOVE.

Michelangelo painted; Beethoven composed; Shakespeare wrote; Mazeroski turned the double play. One of baseball's great viewing pleasures in the 1960s was Bill Mazeroski gliding to second base, taking a toss from the shortstop, pivoting gracefully and in the same fluid motion throwing to first base while leaping just in time to avoid a hard-sliding runner. Many baseball historians regard Mazeroski as the greatest fielding second baseman of all time.

Maz was economy in motion. Infielders normally catch the ball in their glove, then reach in to retrieve it. Not Maz; he used his glove to deflect the ball into his hand. According to Gene Alley, one of Maz's shortstops with the Pittsburgh Pirates: "He had a way of holding his glove at an angle so that the ball would naturally slide out into his throwing hand. Never seen anybody else who could do that, unless it was by accident." Mazeroski is among the few players in the Hall of Fame who was selected primarily for fielding magnificence.

The irony of Mazeroski is that his greatest day in baseball was a result of his bat, not his glove. Of all the home runs in baseball history, only one has ended the seventh game of a World Series, instantly lifting one team and its fans into ecstasy, and plunging the other into agony. Mazeroski struck that blow on October 13, 1960, sending a drive over the left-field wall at Pittsburgh's Forbes Field that gave the Pirates a 10-9 victory over the New York Yankees and their first World Championship in 35 years.

Someone had to break the 9-9 tie that had been forged in the top of the ninth inning when the Yankees scored twice. The 24-year-old Mazeroski seemed an unlikely candidate to be the hero, given that baseball immortals Roberto Clemente, Mickey Mantle, Yogi Berra, 1960 National League batting champ Dick Groat and 1960 American League Most Valuable Player Roger Maris were on the field that afternoon. Mazeroski would complete his career as a mere .260 hitter, though he hit as many as 19 home runs in one season. The first batter in the bottom of the ninth, he took one pitch from Ralph Terry for a ball. Terry next threw a slider that dangled over home plate. Maz took a deep breath and connected solidly. The ball took flight and disappeared over the ivy-covered brick wall, some 365 feet from home plate. Berra, playing left field that day, watched disconsolately. Maz circled the bases quickly, joined by several jubilant fans. Pittsburgh, a Rust Belt city struggling to reinvent itself, erupted in wild celebration for days. A small town triumphed over Gotham, never mind the Yankees outscored the Pirates 55-27 in the Series.

Forbes Field is gone, demolished in 1971 in the name of progress. Yet every October 13 a group of fervent Pirates fans gathers at the exact spot where Mazeroski's home run cleared the ivy. Some celebrations are destined to last forever.

WIN THE BATTLES; LOSE THE WAR
THE YANKEES STATISTICALLY DOMINATED
THE PIRATES IN THE 1960 WORLD SERIES:

YANKEES		PIRATES
	BATTING	
.338	AVERAGE	.256
55	RUNS	27
10	HOME RUNS	4
142	TOTAL BASES	83
	PITCHING	
3.54	ERA	7.11
26	STRIKEOUTS	40

			G	I	S
* BILL MAZEROSKI PITTSBURGH PIRATES	NEW YORK YANKEES	1960	7	9	10-9
* JOE CARTER TORONTO BLUE JAYS	PHILADELPHIA PHILLIES	1993	6	9	8-6
KIRBY PUCKETT MINNESOTA TWINS	ATLANTA BRAVES	1991	6	11	4-3
CARLTON FISK BOSTON RED SOX	CINCINNATI REDS	1975	6	12	7-6
EDDIE MATHEWS MILWAUKEE BRAVES	NEW YORK YANKEES	1957	4	10	7-5
DEREK JETER NEW YORK YANKEES	ARIZONA DIAMONDBACKS	2001	4	10	4-3
MARK McGWIRE OAKLAND ATHLETICS	LOS ANGELES DODGERS	1988	3	9	2-1
CHAD CURTIS NEW YORK YANKEES	ATLANTA BRAVES	1999	3	10	6-5
MICKEY MANTLE NEW YORK YANKEES	ST. LOUIS CARDINALS	1964	3	9	2-1
DUSTY RHODES NEW YORK GIANTS	CLEVELAND INDIANS	1954	1	10	5-2
TOMMY HENRICH NEW YORK YANKEES	BROOKLYN DODGERS	1949	1	9	1-0
KIRK GIBSON LOS ANGELES DODGERS	OAKLAND ATHLETICS	1988	1	9	5-4

* ENDED WORLD SERIES   G: GAME   I: INNING   S: SCORE

I still can't believe it: Mazeroski showed Pirates coach Johnny Pesky,
five years after the feat, where his historic home run cleared the ivy at Forbes Field

(1986)
NEW YORK METS
SCORE AN IMPROBABLE VICTORY IN GAME 6 OF THE WORLD SERIES

The most famous infield grounder in Major League Baseball history glanced off Mookie Wilson's bat, skipped twice, squirted through Bill Buckner's legs and trickled onto the outfield grass, cruelly taunting all of New England with every roll. The sixth game of the 1986 World Series was over, just as soon as Ray Knight raced home to deliver the New York Mets an improbable and astonishing 6-5 victory in the 10th inning. Fifteen minutes earlier, the Mets trailed 5-3, were down to their last out and had nobody on base. The Shea Stadium scoreboard flashed: "Congratulations, Red Sox." Mets first baseman Keith Hernandez retired to the clubhouse to smoke a cigarette and cry in his beer.

Why do these things happen to the Red Sox? Forty years earlier, Johnny Pesky hesitated on a relay throw, enabling Enos Slaughter to com-

plete his mad dash home. Eight years earlier, Bucky Dent struck the blow by homering over the Green Monster. The seventh game in 1986 was played two days after Buckner's error, and when it was over the Red Sox hadn't won the Series in 68 years.

Buckner never should have been on the field in the bottom of the 10th. The 36-year-old first baseman had done his part throughout the summer, providing 18 homers and 102 RBIs, gimping along gamely on ankles so sore that he wore high-cut orthopedic athletic shoes and was scheduled for off-season surgery. Buckner was out there because gruff John McNamara, in his moment of reckoning, showed a sentimental side. The Red Sox manager knew the highest honor a ballplayer could receive was being on the field when his team won the World Series, and no one deserved it more

BEST RECORDS OF THE 1980s

TEAM	YEAR	RECORD	WINNING %	MANAGER	OUTCOME
NEW YORK METS	1986	108-54	.667	DAVEY JOHNSON	WON WORLD SERIES
DETROIT TIGERS	1984	104-58	.642	SPARKY ANDERSON	WON WORLD SERIES
OAKLAND ATHLETICS	1988	104-58	.642	TONY LA RUSSA	LOST WORLD SERIES
NEW YORK YANKEES	1980	103-59	.636	DICK HOWSER	LOST AL CHAMPIONSHIP SERIES
ST. LOUIS CARDINALS	1985	101-61	.623	WHITEY HERZOG	LOST WORLD SERIES
NEW YORK METS	1988	100-60	.625	DAVEY JOHNSON	LOST NL CHAMPIONSHIP SERIES
BALTIMORE ORIOLES	1980	100-62	.617	EARL WEAVER	SECOND PLACE AL EAST

than his wounded soldier Buckner, who usually had deferred to Dave Stapleton when under similar circumstances during the season. As it is, a man who played Major League Baseball for 22 years, had more hits than Joe DiMaggio, Ted Williams or Mickey Mantle — Buckner fell 285 short of 3,000 — and always respected the game and himself, is doomed to be remembered for a ball that stayed down when he anticipated it would pop into his mitt.

Buckner's gaffe has largely obscured the magnificent team that won the Series. The 1986 Mets went 108-54, the best record in Major League Baseball in the 1980s. They smoked the field in the National League East by 21½ games, then withstood the split-fingered brilliance of Houston's Mike Scott in the league championship series. The Mets had the zeal of youth (Darryl Strawberry, Lenny Dykstra, Howard Johnson) and the savvy of veterans (Keith Hernandez, Ray Knight, Gary Carter). The top starting pitchers (Doc Gooden, Bob Ojeda, Sid Fernandez and Ron Darling), all in their 20s, went 66-23. They had a closer for any match-up (righthander Roger McDowell and lefty Jesse Orosco). All that, and it almost was not enough. A small white sphere with red stitches that somehow skipped through the infield rescued the legacy of one team and left the other to ponder the forces that torment it.

REGGIE JACKSON
SLAMS THREE HOME RUNS IN GAME 6 OF THE WORLD SERIES

The New York Yankees were framing a renaissance of their glorious past in the mid-1970s. Aided by the advent of the free-agent players market and owner George Steinbrenner's largesse, the Yankees had a good enough team in place to win the American League pennant in 1976 for the first time in 12 years. But losing the World Series to the Cincinnati Reds in four games pushed the determined Steinbrenner to dig even deeper into his resources. He was the winning bidder for the services of Reggie Jackson, the ranking power hitter of the day and the game's most flamboyant personality.

Amid great fanfare and expectation, Jackson strode into a posh New York hotel on November 29, 1976, took a seat in a gilded chair and

"I must admit: when Reggie hit his third home run and I was sure nobody was looking,

I APPLAUDED IN MY GLOVE."

— STEVE GARVEY, after Game 6 of the 1977 World Series

HOME RUNS			TOTAL BASES			RUNS			SLUGGING AVERAGE			ON-BASE PERCENTAGE		
REGGIE JACKSON NEW YORK (AL)	1977	5	REGGIE JACKSON NEW YORK (AL)	1977	25	REGGIE JACKSON NEW YORK (AL)	1977	10	LOU GEHRIG NEW YORK (AL)	1928	1.727	LOU GEHRIG NEW YORK (AL)	1928	2.433
WILLIE AIKENS KANSAS CITY	1980	4	WILLIE STARGELL PITTSBURGH	1979	25	PAUL MOLITOR TORONTO	1993	10	BABE RUTH NEW YORK (AL)	1928	1.375	BABE RUTH NEW YORK (AL)	1928	2.022
HANK BAUER NEW YORK (AL)	1958	4	LOU BROCK ST. LOUIS	1968	24	LENNY DYKSTRA PHILADELPHIA	1993	9	HANK GOWDY BOSTON (NL)	1914	1.273	HANK GOWDY BOSTON (NL)	1914	1.960
LENNY DYKSTRA PHILADELPHIA	1993	4	PAUL MOLITOR TORONTO	1952	24	LOU GEHRIG NEW YORK (AL)	1928	9	REGGIE JACKSON NEW YORK (AL)	1977	1.250	REGGIE JACKSON NEW YORK (AL)	1977	1.772
LOU GEHRIG NEW YORK (AL)	1928	4	DUKE SNIDER BROOKLYN	1952	24	ROY WHITE NEW YORK (AL)	1978	9	CHARLIE KELLER NEW YORK (AL)	1939	1.188	LOU GEHRIG NEW YORK (AL)	1932	1.697
BABE RUTH NEW YORK (AL)	1926	4												
DUKE SNIDER BROOKLYN	1955	4												
DUKE SNIDER BROOKLYN	1952	4												
GENE TENACE OAKLAND	1972	4												

INDIVIDUAL WORLD SERIES ACHIEVEMENT

"In the building I live in on Park Avenue there are 10 people who could buy the Yankees,

BUT NOT ONE OF THEM COULD HIT THE BALL OUT OF YANKEE STADIUM."

— REGGIE JACKSON

signed what then was the most lucrative contract in baseball history: $2.9 million for five years. Never short on self-promotion, he remarked that he probably would have a candy bar named after him.

Jackson's adjustment to a Yankees team rife with seasoned veterans resentful of his celebrity and managed by fiery Billy Martin proved to be a summer-long ordeal. Jackson certainly didn't endear himself to his new clubhouse when he told a magazine writer prior to the season, "I'm the straw that stirs the drink," adding that respected team captain Thurman Munson "thinks he can be the straw that stirs the drink, but he can only stir it bad."

Yet when they took the field, the Yankees managed to put aside their differences and perform as one. Jackson, most of all, relished the refuge he found four or five times a night when he strode to home plate and cocked his menacing bat. He achieved one of his best seasons — 32 home runs, 110 runs batted in, 20 game-winning hits — and the Yankees again advanced to the World Series, this time against the Los Angeles Dodgers.

After five games, the Yankees held a 3-2 lead and Jackson had two home runs. As the teams prepared for Game 6 at Yankee Stadium on October 18, Jackson was a man possessed during batting practice, blasting pitch after pitch into the seats. "Save some of those for the game," said Willie Randolph. Jackson shot a glare at his teammate and said defiantly, "There are more where those came from." Were there ever. During the next three hours, Jackson put on the greatest show ever by a batter in the World Series. After walking in his first at-bat, he drilled home runs on the first pitch in each of his next three trips to the plate. The third home run was a majestic blast that soared like a rocket toward center field, cleared the fence and bounced crazily among the black unoccupied seats — more than 450 feet from home plate. As Jackson circled the bases in his signature swaggering trot, the crowd of 56,407 was deafening in its "Reggie! Reggie! Reggie!" salute. Twenty minutes later, the Yankees clinched their first World Championship since 1962.

Jackson's five home runs — and fourth in four official at-bats going back to the eighth inning of Game 5 — is a record for a World Series. As great a player as he was, he rose to a higher level when performing in October on baseball's grandest stage. Jackson's batting average for his six World Series is 95 points better than his season average (.357 to .262) and his slugging average of .755 is a Series record.

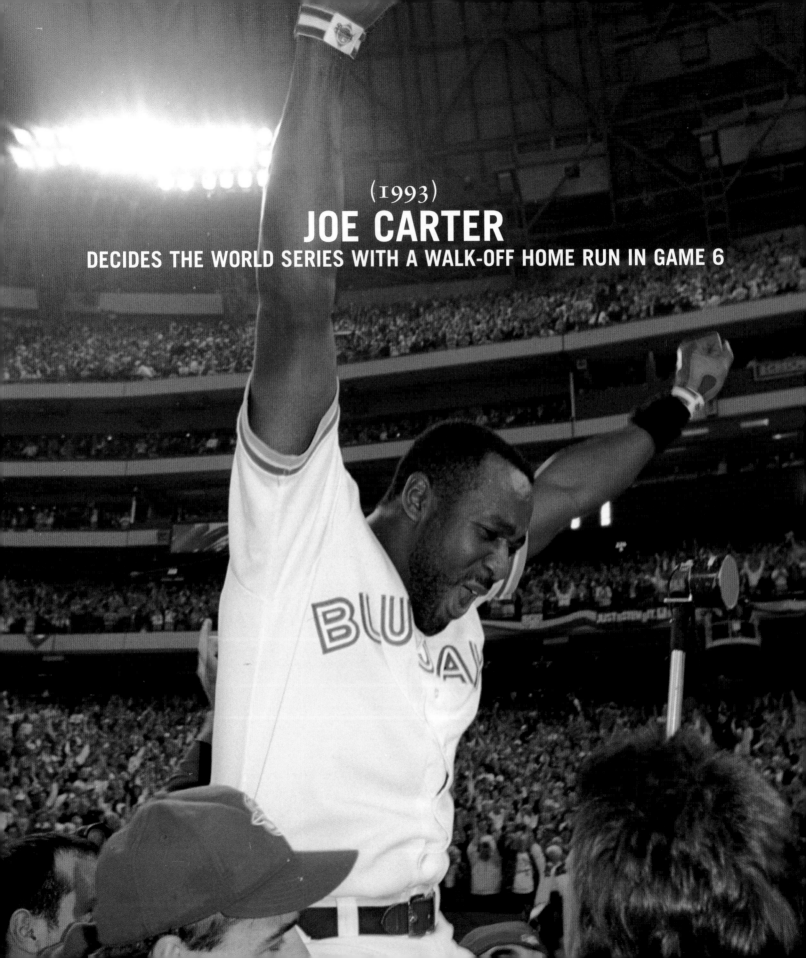

(1993)
JOE CARTER
DECIDES THE WORLD SERIES WITH A WALK-OFF HOME RUN IN GAME 6

Failure is the closest thing to reality for a hitter, yet as always in these situations it
WAS THE FURTHEST THING FROM CARTER'S MIND.

Joe Carter did two things more consistently than anyone else of his era in Major League Baseball: produce RBIs and make outs. He was a veritable RBI-machine from 1986 through 1997, driving home no fewer than 102 runs in 10 of those 12 seasons. Only eight other players — among them Ruth, Gehrig, Mays, Aaron — can lay claim to 10 100-RBI seasons, and all are in the Hall of Fame. Carter became a prolific RBI-man by affording himself plenty of opportunity. He played in 97 percent of his team's games over those 12 seasons and almost always batted third, fourth or fifth in the lineup — optimum conditions for producing runs. The more opportunity for success,

the more opportunity for failure, too, especially in the case of a career .259 hitter. Carter made an average of 483 outs in his 100-RBI seasons, more than anyone else playing at the time. Yet the smartest teams value most those players who can endure the daily grind of a six-month marathon and keep a steady pace — and that was Joe Carter defined.

The Toronto Blue Jays started winning in 1983, the seventh year of their existence, but the big payoffs didn't come for them until Carter joined the team in 1991 and became their cleanup hitter. The Blue Jays won the World Series in 1992 and were back again a year later, this time against the

Philadelphia Phillies. The 1992 Series initially became a memorable event when the Blue Jays beat the Phillies 15-14 in Game 4 — the highest-scoring game in the 532-game history of the World Series. The Phillies won later that day, reducing Toronto's lead to three games to two, and back in Toronto for Game 6 they took an 8-6 lead into the bottom of the ninth inning. Mitch Williams, the "Wild Thing", was pitching, two Blue Jays were on base, one out had been recorded, and it was Carter's turn to bat. This was Joe's time, where he wanted to be, what he was paid for, what he was about as a ballplayer. Failure is the closest thing to reality for a hitter, yet as always in these situations it was the furthest thing from Carter's mind.

Williams got the count to 2-and-2, then tried to finish Carter with a slider. But Carter was ready, connecting bat to ball with his big, muscular arms and letting the resulting momentum do the rest of the work. The ball landed well over the left-field fence at Skydome, and the Blue Jays were champions again. Carter, in a state of delirium, hopped and danced around the bases and into baseball lore. It marked the first time a World Series had ended on a come-from-behind home run. (The score was tied when Bill Mazeroski's Game 7 home run ended the 1960 Series.) Carter was in the right place at the right time — that is all anyone can ask for. The rest is up to them, and those who best understand failure are often in the best position to succeed.

TEAMS THAT WON THE WORLD SERIES IN THE BOTTOM OF THE LAST INNING

YEAR	WINNING TEAM	G	S	I	HOW IT ENDED	LOSING TEAM
2001	ARIZONA DIAMONDBACKS	7	3-2	9	LUIS GONZALEZ'S ONE-RUN SINGLE WITH ONE OUT	NEW YORK YANKEES
1997	FLORIDA MARLINS	7	3-2	11	EDGAR RENTERIA'S ONE-RUN SINGLE WITH TWO OUTS	CLEVELAND INDIANS
1993	TORONTO BLUE JAYS	6	8-6	9	JOE CARTER'S THREE-RUN HOMER WITH ONE OUT	PHILADELPHIA PHILLIES
1991	MINNESOTA TWINS	7	1-0	10	GENE LARKIN'S ONE-RUN SINGLE WITH ONE OUT	ATLANTA BRAVES
1960	PITTSBURGH PIRATES	7	10-9	9	BILL MAZEROSKI'S ONE-RUN HOME RUN WITH NO OUTS	NEW YORK YANKEES
1953	NEW YORK YANKEES	6	4-3	9	BILLY MARTIN'S ONE-RUN SINGLE WITH ONE OUT	BROOKLYN DODGERS
1935	DETROIT TIGERS	6	4-3	0	GOOSE GOSLIN'S ONE-RUN SINGLE WITH TWO OUTS	CHICAGO CUBS
1929	PHILADELPHIA ATHLETICS	5	3-2	9	BING MILLER'S ONE-RUN DOUBLE WITH TWO OUTS	CHICAGO CUBS
1927	NEW YORK YANKEES	4	4-3	9	EARLE COMBS SCORED ON A WILD PITCH WITH TWO OUTS	PITTSBURGH PIRATES
1924	WASHINGTON SENATORS	7	4-3	12	EARL McNELLY'S ONE-RUN SINGLE WITH ONE OUT	NEW YORK GIANTS
1912	BOSTON RED SOX	7	3-2	10	LARRY GARDNER'S SACRIFICE FLY WITH ONE OUT	NEW YORK GIANTS

G: GAME   S: SCORE   I: INNING

ROBERTO CLEMENTE
ACHIEVES HIS 3,000TH HIT IN HIS FINAL AT-BAT

"What did he hit?" Don Drysdale once was asked after giving up a home run to Clemente.

"BALL FOUR," DRYSDALE SAID.

R oberto Clemente never got old. He never became an aging ballplayer, fighting the ravages of time, incapable of the magnificent feats of his youth. The mind's images are of a dashing, daring, defiant, proud ballplayer — "The Great One," Puerto Rico's most-revered son, golden rightfielder of the Pittsburgh Pirates, frozen in his prime.

We remember Clemente at bat, constantly rolling his neck, stretching his back, grimacing, as if the pain was almost too much to bear. Then the man who knew no strike zone would reach for a pitch six inches off home plate and drive it on a sizzling line into the gap, running like the wind and streaking into second base, a thin smile pursing his lips. "What did he hit?" Don Drysdale once was asked after giving up a home run to Clemente. "Ball four," Drysdale said.

We remember Clemente in right field, fielding the ball nonchalantly,

dangling it casually at his side. This was his standing dare to every baserunner: "Seeing as how this is the most powerful arm ever attached to a Major League Baseball outfielder, and it will blow you clean off the basepaths, you gotta ask yourself: 'Do I feel lucky?' Well, do you, punk? Go ahead — make my day." Few challenged the legendary Clemente hose. In Game 6 of the 1971 World Series, Merv Rettenmund was leading off third base when Frank Robinson lofted a 300-foot fly to right field. Clemente, all in the same motion, caught the ball, spun a half turn and delivered the ball to home plate. Rettenmund rolled his eyes and retreated meekly to third.

When discussing baseball's superstars in the 1960s, those outside of Pittsburgh were apt to omit Clemente from the elite group of Willie Mays, Mickey Mantle and Hank Aaron. Yet Clemente's sustained excellence was equally impressive. He won four batting titles, 12 Gold Gloves and two

GAMES NEEDED TO REACH 3,000 HITS

PLAYER	GAMES TO 3,000	AGE	CAREER HITS
TY COBB	2,135	34	4,189
NAP LAJOIE	2,224	39	3,242
TONY GWYNN	2,284	39	3,141
STAN MUSIAL	2,301	37	3,630
PAUL WANER	2,314	39	3,152
HONUS WAGNER	2,332	40	3,415
TRIS SPEAKER	2,341	37	3,514
PETE ROSE	2,370	37	4,256
PAUL MOLITOR	2,411	40	3,319
ROD CAREW	2,417	39	3,053
WADE BOGGS	2,430	41	3,010
ROBERTO CLEMENTE	2,433	38	3,000
HANK AARON	2,460	36	3,771
EDDIE COLLINS	2,505	38	3,315
GEORGE BRETT	2,559	39	3,154
LOU BROCK	2,629	40	3,023
WILLIE MAYS	2,639	39	3,283
ROBIN YOUNT	2,708	36	3,142
EDDIE MURRAY	2,764	39	3,255
CAL RIPKEN JR.	2,800	39	3,184
AL KALINE	2,825	39	3,007
DAVE WINFIELD	2,840	41	3,110
CARL YASTRZEMSKI	2,848	40	3,419
* RICKEY HENDERSON	2,979	42	3,000
CAP ANSON	UNKNOWN	45	3,418

* STILL ACTIVE, TOTALS THROUGH 2001

IT WAS CLASSIC CLEMENTE —
a ringing double into the gap at Three Rivers Stadium in Pittsburgh on September 30, 1972. It was his final at-bat of the regular season, and after 5 games in the National League playoffs,
HE HAD NO MORE AT-BATS REMAINING ON EARTH.

World Series championship rings. For those who didn't fully comprehend the breadth of his talent, Clemente put on a show in the 1971 Series as dazzling as there ever has been on baseball's biggest stage. A year later he became a true immortal by becoming the 11th player ever to achieve 3,000 hits. It was classic Clemente — a ringing double into the gap at Three Rivers Stadium in Pittsburgh on September 30, 1972. It was his final at-bat of the regular season, and after five games in the National League playoffs, he had no more at-bats remaining on earth.

Three months later Clemente was dead, killed on New Year's Eve in an airplane crash off the coast of Puerto Rico. As amazing as his play on the field

was, Clemente had an even greater capacity for humanitarianism. So it surprised no one that he was the driving force behind a Puerto Rican relief effort to gather food and clothing for survivors of an earthquake that had devastated Nicaragua. The overloaded DC-7 bearing eight tons of goods, Clemente and four others sputtered after takeoff and crashed into the Caribbean Sea. Manny Sanguillen, the young Pirates catcher who idolized Clemente, rushed to the crash site. Over and over, the distraught Sanguillen dove into the 30-foot water, searching and despairing, bearing the grief of Pittsburgh and Puerto Rico with him in each plunge. Clemente's body was never found. He was gone at 38, forever young.

(1938)
JOHNNY VANDER MEER
PITCHES TWO CONSECUTIVE NO-HITTERS

Johnny Vander Meer held exceptional promise when he joined the Cincinnati Reds in 1937. The strong, wiry lefthander threw a blazing fastball and a biting curveball, but he didn't put nearly enough of his pitches in the strike zone. During spring training the following year, a Reds coach suggested to Vander Meer that he study the pitching style of Lefty Grove, the great Boston Red Sox lefthander, and try to emulate him. Vander Meer eagerly followed the advice and made adjustments on the mound that alleviated his wildness and earned him a regular turn in the Reds pitching rotation.

By June 1938 Vander Meer had won five games and was leading the National League in strikeouts — superb work, but hardly an omen of the incredible feat he was about to achieve. Vander Meer pitched a no-hitter against the Boston Bees on June 11 and four days later followed it with a no-hitter against the Brooklyn Dodgers.

There were 205 no-hitters pitched in the major leagues from 1900 through 2001, 58 before Vander Meer and 145 after him. Nolan Ryan pitched seven of those no-hitters, and Sandy Koufax pitched four. Yet neither of them, nor anyone else, matched Vander Meer's feat. Only one has even come close. In 1947, Ewell Blackwell of the Reds pitched a no-hitter against the Boston Braves — formerly the Bees — and in his next start held the Dodgers hitless until the ninth inning. Not a man to boast, Vander Meer was merely stating the obvious years later when he remarked: "I think my record and Joe DiMaggio's 56-game hitting streak are just about the two toughest records to break."

1938

LOWEST BATTING AVERAGE AGAINST A PITCHER

JOHNNY VANDER MEER CINCINNATI REDS	.213
BOB FELLER CLEVELAND INDIANS	.220
RUSS BAUERS PITTSBURGH PIRATES	.233
CLAY BRYANT CHICAGO CUBS	.235
JOHNNY ALLEN CLEVELAND INDIANS	.246
DANNY MacFAYDEN BOSTON BEES	.247
HAL SCHUMACHER NEW YORK GIANTS	.248
CARL HUBBELL NEW YORK GIANTS	.249
BILL LEE CHICAGO CUBS	.252
BOB KLINGER PITTSBURGH PIRATES	.253

PITCHERS WITH TWO OR MORE NO-HITTERS SINCE 1900

NOLAN RYAN	7	STEVE BUSBY	2	DUTCH LEONARD	2	WARREN SPAHN	2
SANDY KOUFAX	4	CARL ERSKINE	2	JIM MALONEY	2	BILL STONEMAN	2
LARRY CORCORAN	3	BOB FORSCH	2	CHRISTY MATHEWSON	2	VIRGIL TRUCKS	2
BOB FELLER	3	PUD GALVIN	2	HIDEO NOMO	2	JOHNNY VANDER MEER	2
CY YOUNG	3	KEN HOLTZMAN	2	ALLIE REYNOLDS	2	ED WALSH	2
JIM BUNNING	2	ADDIE JOSS	2	FRANK SMITH	2	DON WILSON	2

Vander Meer's second no-hitter came in the first night game ever played at Ebbets Field. The Dodgers seized the opportunity to turn the evening into a grand event, staging elaborate festivities before the game, including an exhibition race that featured the Olympic sprint champion Jesse Owens. The Brooklyn park, crowded beyond its 38,000 capacity, including more than 500 people from Vander Meer's New Jersey hometown, was charged with excitement and anticipation.

Still, the 23-year-old pitcher kept his nerve, even after walking three consecutive batters with one out in the ninth inning. After a visit from Reds manager Bill McKechnie, who told him to "just relax and throw naturally," Vander Meer got the second out on an infield grounder. Up next was Leo Durocher, who lifted a fly ball to center field that nestled into the glove of Harry Craft for one of the most famous outs in major league history.

(1991)

JACK MORRIS

PITCHES 10 SCORELESS INNINGS IN GAME 7 OF THE WORLD SERIES

PITCHERS WHO HAVE ACHIEVED SHUTOUTS IN GAME 7 OF THE WORLD SERIES						
* JACK MORRIS	1991	MINNESOTA	1	ATLANTA	0	7-HITTER
BRET SABERHAGEN	1985	KANSAS CITY	11	ST. LOUIS	0	5-HITTER
SANDY KOUFAX	1965	LOS ANGELES	2	MINNESOTA	0	3-HITTER
RALPH TERRY	1962	NEW YORK (AL)	1	SAN FRANCISCO	0	4-HITTER
LEW BURDETTE	1957	MILWAUKEE	5	NEW YORK (AL)	0	7-HITTER
JOHNNY KUCKS	1956	NEW YORK (AL)	9	BROOKLYN	0	3-HITTER
JOHNNY PODRES	1955	BROOKLYN	2	NEW YORK (AL)	0	8-HITTER
DIZZY DEAN	1934	ST. LOUIS (NL)	11	DETROIT	0	6-HITTER
BABE ADAMS	1909	PITTSBURGH	8	DETROIT	0	6-HITTER

* 10 INNINGS

HE WAS AS TOUGH AS THEY COME,

relished the competition, always wanted the ball and usually put up an argument

WHEN ASKED TO GIVE IT UP TO A FRESH HAND.

Jack Morris's bushy moustache and piercing glare afforded him the appearance of a gunslinger in the old West, and he went about his work in the manner of a man whose life depended on it. Morris was not the fastest, cleverest or most dominating pitcher of his era. He never won the Cy Young award, and his career 3.90 ERA is the highest among the 42 pitchers who won at least 250 games. For Morris, the point was winning, and from 1979 through 1992 he did that far better than any other pitcher, racking up 233 victories, 41 more than second-place Bob Welch. He was the front man in the rotation for teams in Detroit, Minnesota and Toronto that won the World Series. He was as tough as they come, relished the competition, always wanted the ball and usually put up an argument when asked to give it up to a fresh hand. Typical of Morris was his curt statement on the eve of Game 7 of the 1991 World Series, his to pitch for the Minnesota Twins. "Let's get it on!" he grunted, already screwing on his game-face.

The 1991 World Series, by some accounts, was the greatest ever played. The Twins were wringing the last drops from a formidable nucleus that had won the 1987 Series. The long-suffering Atlanta Braves had empowered themselves with brilliant pitching and were blooming into the National League's team of the 1990s. That both participants had finished in last place the previous season further stoked passion and frenzy in the two cities.

"I don't know where the strength came from. My arm was alive. **THE BASEBALL GODS IN THE SKY MUST HAVE BLESSED ME TONIGHT.**"
— JACK MORRIS

Metrodome fans madly waved Homer Hankies and raised the roof to jet-engine decibel levels. Atlanta Fulton County Stadium fans tomahawk-chopped at a delirious pace. Five of the games were decided by one run, four were decided on the last pitch, three required extra innings. Game 6 was one for the ages. The bear-sized Kirby Puckett climbed the Plexiglas in center field and robbed the Braves of a home run, then won the game 4-3 with a homer of his own in the bottom of the 11th inning. "And we'll see you tomorrow night," said Jack Buck in a marvelous monotone on CBS-TV.

Game 7 pitted 36-year-old Morris against 24-year-old John Smoltz, a Michigan native who had idolized Morris during Morris's salad days with the Tigers. They matched zero for zero on the scoreboard until Smoltz dropped out in the eighth inning. Morris, who would have given up a run in the eighth except for Lonnie Smith's base-running gaffe, soldiered on through the ninth, the score still 0-0. Upon returning to the dugout, the pitcher was confronted by manager Tom Kelly. "That's enough, Jack." Morris replied, "I'm fine." "Are you sure?" Kelly pressed. "I said I was fine. If I wasn't fine, I'd tell you," Morris snapped, his fire at full stoke. He retired the Braves again in the 10th, then the Twins scored a run and it was over. No one doubted that Morris would have been back out on the mound for the 11th, for as long as it took. No one was taking the ball away from him on this night, one of the grandest in baseball history.

SATCHEL PAIGE

BECOMES THE FIRST PLAYER INDUCTED INTO THE HALL OF FAME FOR HIS NEGRO LEAGUE ACCOMPLISHMENTS

Satchel Paige stood 6-foot-3 and carried but 180 pounds on legs so spindly that he wore two pair of long, thick socks to fill the slack in his baseball pants. His arms were equally long and spare. This man struck an unremarkable appearance on a pitcher's mound, and he appeared ungainly as he took a windup, kicked his left leg and delivered a baseball toward home plate. What happened next, though, set Paige apart from per- haps 98 percent of those who have been called pitchers. His fast offerings darted over home plate, moving left, right or down, but never true. His slower pitches curved impossibly or tantalized maddeningly. All were amazed by his unerring control, though Satch hardly considered the condi- tion to be extraordinary. "Just take the ball and throw it where you want to," he always said. "Throw strikes. Home plate don't move."

SATCHEL'S RULES FOR THE GOOD LIFE

(As printed on the back of his business card.)

1. Avoid fried foods cause they angers up the blood.

2. If your stomach disputes you, lay down and pacify it with cool thoughts.

3. Keep the juices flowin' by janglin 'round gently as you move.

4. Go very light on vices such as carryin' on in society. The social ramble just ain't restful.

5. Avoid runnin' at all times.

6. Don't ever look back. Somethin' might be gainin'.

Paige was so proud of his pitches that he named them. He developed a repertoire all his own, never to be duplicated. He threw Long Tom (best fastball) and Little Tom (medium fastball), the Bee Ball ("It be where I want it to be"), the Two-Hump Blooper (ultraslow change-up), the Barber (guaranteed to graze a batter's chin) and his famous hesitation pitch, unleashed after he froze in mid-delivery. He had a hypnotic personality and a flamboyant manner about him. At the peak of his career, he was baseball's best drawing card since Babe Ruth. We did not say Major League Baseball's. Paige was an African-American, which relegated him to the Negro Leagues for more than 20 years. His legendary feats attracted huge crowds, mostly African-American people during the summer season. The rest of the year, Paige and other Negro League players toured the country and took on all comers, oftentimes all-star teams comprised of Major League Baseball players. Black and white fans alike, heavy with anticipation, turned out in large numbers, and as often as not the Negro League team won with Paige out-dueling the likes of Dizzy Dean or Bob Feller.

Those exhibitions generated a financial windfall of such impact that social segregation soon was outweighed by economic logic in Major League Baseball. Jackie Robinson in 1947 became the first African-American player in the major leagues since the late 1800s. Paige had hoped to be the first, and he surely deserved the honor, but by then he was 40 years old and much of the electricity had drained from his right arm. He was summoned a year later by the Cleveland Indians owner, Bill Veeck, who knew he was doing the right thing even if ol' Satch had nothing left. That proved to be far from the case. Relying on savvy, guile and off-speed pitches delivered from an endless array of windups and arm angles, Paige earned his keep in Major League

THE WISDOM OF SATCHEL PAIGE

"Age is a case of mind over matter. If you don't mind, it don't matter."

"Ain't no man can avoid being born average, but there ain't no man got to be common."

"How old would you be if you didn't know how old you were?"

"Work like you don't need the money. Love like you've never been hurt. Dance like nobody's watching."

THE WIT OF SATCHEL PAIGE

"I ain't never had a job, I just always played baseball."

"I never threw an illegal pitch. The trouble is,
once in a while I toss one that ain't never been seen by this generation."

"I use my single windup, my double windup, my triple windup, my hesitation windup, my no windup.
I also use my step-n-pitch-it, my submariner, my sidearmer, and my bat dodger.
Man's got to do what he's got to do."

"One time Cool Papa Bell hit a line drive right past my ear. I turned around and saw
the ball hit his ass sliding into second."

Paige relaxed in a recliner provided for his comfort in the St. Louis Browns bullpen.

Boxing champion Joe Louis was among Paige's admirers.

"Just take the ball and throw it where you want to.
THROW STRIKES. HOME PLATE DON'T MOVE."

Baseball for five seasons, leaving after the 1953 season. He wasn't quite done. The Kansas City Athletics of his adopted hometown brought him back in 1965 for one game. Paige was 59, and he pitched three scoreless innings against the Boston Red Sox, yielding only one hit, a double by Carl Yastrzemski.

It is estimated that Paige pitched in more than 2,000 games during the 1930s and 1940s. Except for his time in Major League Baseball (28 victories, 31 losses, 3.29 earned-run average) there is no universally accepted record of his accomplishments. But those who were there

knew: He almost always was the best player on the field. That is why in 1971 Paige was accorded the honor of being the first player from the Negro League elected to the National Baseball Hall of Fame. Justice came late in his life, but nonetheless it came. Satch called the induction ceremonies in Cooperstown "the proudest day of my life," and he even got a little humble in his speech, remarking that there had been a lot of Satchel Paiges in the Negro League, men who had been his equal. That, of course, was not true. He broke the mold, and in many ways he broke the color line.

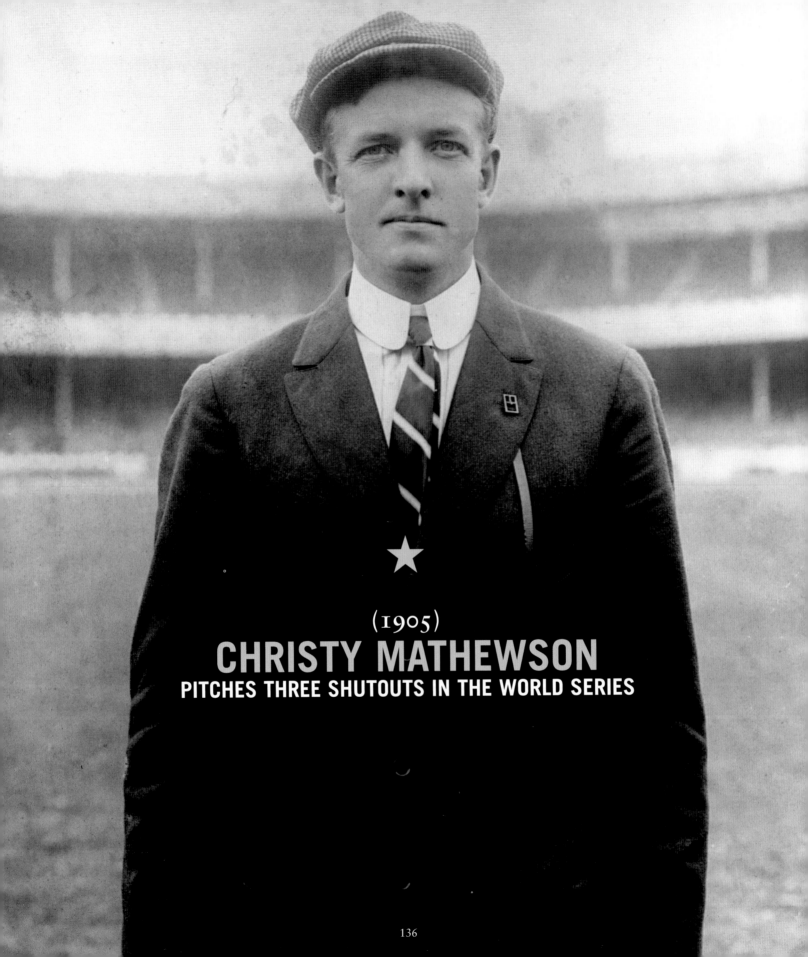

(1905)

CHRISTY MATHEWSON

PITCHES THREE SHUTOUTS IN THE WORLD SERIES

★★★★★

CHRISTY MATHEWSON
brought something to baseball no one else had ever given the game.
He handed the game a certain

TOUCH OF CLASS,

an indefinable lift in
CULTURE, BRAINS, AND PERSONALITY.

—GRANTLAND RICE, sportswriter

★★★★★

Baseball had woven itself into the American fabric by the early 1900s, yet the masses embraced ballplayers only between the white lines. The game's stars generally were social pariahs, hard-drinking, fast-living yahoos too crude and boisterous for civilized company.

Christy Mathewson was a welcome exception, the first professional sports star to be viewed as a hero and an exemplary role model. College-educated, refined and charismatic, he carried himself in a stately manner on and off the field. Mathewson sang in the glee club, belonged to

premier pitchers during the first two decades of the 1900s. Mathewson joined the New York Giants in 1900, and when his 17-year career had run its course — all but the final two months spent with the Giants — he had 373 victories (third best all time) and a 2.13 ERA (eighth best). He won at least 30 games in each of four seasons, and never won fewer than 20 for 12 consecutive years (1903–1914).

The redoubtable Mathewson had three superior pitches: the requisite fastball and curveball, and a "fadeaway" that he called his magic pitch.

Every great ballplayer has a defining moment,
AND MATHEWSON'S CAME IN THE 1905 WORLD SERIES.

a literary society, married his college sweetheart and was always true to her. He once declined a tidy sum to endorse a Broadway drinking and dancing hall — the owners wanted to rename it "The Christy Mathewson" — telling his mother, "If I had to make money that way I wouldn't want any." He was strikingly handsome, too, a strapping lad at 6-foot-1, 190 pounds with fine features, blue eyes and blond hair.

And could he ever pitch. Mathewson and Walter Johnson were the

The "fadeaway"— a screwball in modern-day terminology — broke in to right-handed hitters, eating up their hands. Mathewson had exquisite control of all his pitches, averaging but 1.6 walks per nine innings for his career. He often went through nine innings having thrown fewer than 80 pitches.

Every great ballplayer has a defining moment, and Mathewson's came in the 1905 World Series. The Series went five games, all shutouts — the only World Series in which every one of the games was decided by a shutout. The

CHRISTY

My eyes are very misty,
As I pen these lines to Christy,
Oh my heart is full of heaviness today.
May the flowers never wither, Matty,
On your grave in Cincinnati,
Which you've chosen for your final fadeaway.

—RING LARDNER, New York sportswriter,
after Mathewson was traded to Cincinnati, where
he spent the final two months of his career

MOST WORLD SERIES SHUTOUTS

PITCHER	TIME PERIOD	NO.
CHRISTY MATHEWSON NEW YORK GIANTS	1905–1913	4
THREE FINGER BROWN CHICAGO CUBS	1906–1908	3
WHITEY FORD NEW YORK YANKEES	1960–1961	3
BILL DINEEN BOSTON RED SOX	1903	2
ART NEHF NEW YORK GIANTS	1921–1923	2
BILL HALLAHAN ST. LOUIS CARDINALS	1930–1931	2
ALLIE REYNOLDS NEW YORK YANKEES	1949–1952	2
LEW BURDETTE MILWAUKEE BRAVES	1957	2
SANDY KOUFAX LOS ANGELES DODGERS	1965	2
BOB GIBSON ST. LOUIS CARDINALS	1967–1968	2

ear-old Mathewson went to the mound in Game 1, Game 3 and the
sive Game 5, and every time he walked off after nine innings having
yielded a run to Connie Mack's American League champion
adelphia Athletics. The scores: 3-0, 9-0 and 2-0. In 27 innings over a
day period, Mathewson gave up 14 hits, walked one and struck out 18

Befitting his standards for citizenship, Mathewson joined th
1918 to fight in World War I. He was exposed to poison gas in
suffered lung damage that would develop into tuberculosis and t
He died at age 47 on the opening day of the 1925 World Series, an
20 years earlier he had dominated like no one before or since

(1991)
RICKEY HENDERSON
BREAKS LOU BROCK'S ALL-TIME STOLEN BASE RECORD

The rabbits first appeared in the 1970s and quickly multiplied. Major League Baseball teams needed them to chase fly balls in the cavernous stadiums that were sprouting up around the country. The new parks were so big and the artificial playing surfaces so fast that some teams found rabbits to be more valuable than home run hitters. The game zoomed into the fast lane. Vince Coleman, Ron LeFlore, Omar Moreno, Tim Raines, Willie Wilson, Dave Collins, Rudy Law, Bill North, Otis Nixon, Alan Wiggins were the rabbits that ran. They stole bases by the 70s, the 80s, the 90s, and even the 100s. None, though, could keep pace with Rickey Henderson, who not only stole bases but did it with style, swagger and defiance.

Henderson was cut from a different bolt than the other rabbits. He had the physique of an NFL running back, compact and powerful, steeled in the chest and legs. He could put a jolt in the ball when he connected, and no other batter in the game was better at drawing Ball Four. He often referred to himself in the third person ("Rickey, Rickey, you're so fine, you blow my mind.") and was known to talk to his bats ("Which one of you bad boys got some hits in you?"). Henderson wasn't as fast as many of the other rabbits, but none had his explosion off the mark; that was his edge over 30 yards, the only sprint that mattered. Henderson carefully measured his lead off first base, took off as if shot out of a cannon, swooshed into second in a head-first slide, then broke into his smug "Ain't Rickey amazin' " chuckle as he dusted himself off. The dash from second to steal third was just as easy for him. When he was 23, Henderson did this so frequently and so well that by the end of the 1982 season he had stolen 130 bases, 12 more than Lou Brock's previous Major League Baseball record.

141

MOST STOLEN BASES IN ONE SEASON SINCE 1900					
RICKEY HENDERSON OAKLAND ATHLETICS	130	1982	RICKEY HENDERSON OAKLAND ATHLETICS	100	1980
LOU BROCK ST. LOUIS CARDINALS	118	1974	RON LeFLORE DETROIT TIGERS	97	1980
VINCE COLEMAN ST. LOUIS CARDINALS	110	1985	TY COBB DETROIT TIGERS	96	1915
VINCE COLEMAN ST. LOUIS CARDINALS	109	1987	OMAR MORENO PITTSBURGH PIRATES	96	1980
RICKEY HENDERSON OAKLAND ATHLETICS	108	1983	MAURY WILLS LOS ANGELES DODGERS	94	1965
VINCE COLEMAN ST. LOUIS CARDINALS	107	1986	RICKEY HENDERSON NEW YORK YANKEES	93	1988
MAURY WILLS LOS ANGELES DODGERS	104	1962	TIM RAINES MONTREAL EXPOS	90	1983

"It wasn't until I saw Rickey that I understood what baseball was about.

RICKEY HENDERSON IS A RUN, MAN. THAT'S IT.

If he's with you, that's great. If he's not, you won't like it."

★★★

— MITCHELL PAGE, Major League Baseball player, 1977–1984

Henderson carefully measured his lead off first base, took off as if shot out of a cannon, swooshed into second in a headfirst slide, then broke into his smug

"AIN'T RICKEY AMAZIN' "

chuckle as he dusted himself off.

Career achievement records are supposed to be set by legendary players winding down illustrious careers. Yet Henderson was just 32, fully in his prime, when he dashed off second base at the Oakland Coliseum on May 2, 1991, hell-bent for third. When he slid in safely, he had 939 stolen bases, the all-time record, also taking this mark from Brock. Never the shrinking violet, Henderson lifted his record-setting base above his head and with Ali-like pretension proclaimed to a full house, which included Brock: "Today I am the greatest of all time."

The rabbits died out after the next round of stadium construction, when retro-look, intimate parks became all the rage. Pop flies that carried into the cheap seats of the new bandboxes made fleet feet obsolete. Henderson, though, carried on, year after year, team after team, into his

40s. Among season totals for stolen bases, he has seven of the top 30. At the outset of the 2002 season, he had 1,395 stolen bases — 34 percent more than Brock in second place. No other man had a firmer grip on a Major League Baseball record, not even Nolan Ryan, who had 28 percent more strikeouts than Steve Carlton, next on that list.

This fact might be even more amazing: Henderson had at least twice as many stolen bases as all but nine others in history. And in some minds, stolen bases are regarded as the least of Henderson's feats. He also broke Ty Cobb's Major League Baseball career record for runs and Babe Ruth's record for walks, hit the most home runs leading off a game, and is one of 25 who has achieved 3,000 hits. A fast man among fast company.

A LEAGUE OF HIS OWN

erms of the distance between first place and second place, Rickey Henderson's career rec
for stolen bases is the most impressive in Major League Baseball history. Following are
record holders and their percentage lead over second place.

	RECORD HOLDER	RECORD	SECOND PLACE	RECORD	DIFFERENCE
STOLEN BASES	RICKEY HENDERSON	1,395	LOU BROCK	938	.34
STRIKEOUTS	NOLAN RYAN	5,714	STEVE CARLTON	4,136	.28
HITTING STREAK	JOE DiMAGGIO	56	PETE ROSE	44	.23
VICTORIES	CY YOUNG	522	WALTER JOHNSON	417	.18
SAVES	LEE SMITH	478	JOHN FRANCO	422	.12
TOTAL BASES	HANK AARON	6,856	STAN MUSIAL	6,134	.11
HOME RUNS	HANK AARON	755	BABE RUTH	714	.05
RBIs	HANK AARON	2,297	BABE RUTH	2,213	.04
HITS	PETE ROSE	4,256	TY COBB	4,189	.02

STATISTICS ARE THROUGH THE 2001 SEASON

(2001)

ICHIRO
CROSSES THE PACIFIC, WINS TWO MAJOR AWARDS,
AND IS THE FANS' TOP CHOICE FOR THE ALL-STAR GAME

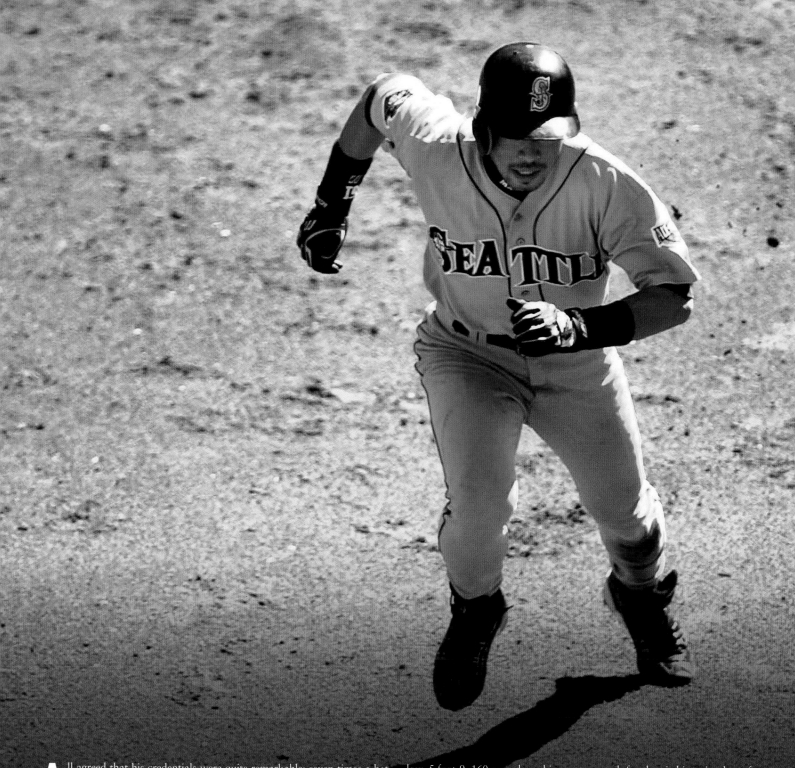

All agreed that his credentials were quite remarkable: seven times a batting champion; 210 hits in a 130-game season; on base safely in 69 consecutive games; 216 consecutive at-bats without striking out; three MVP awards; seven Gold Gloves. No doubt, Ichiro Suzuki was the scourge of all Japanese pitchers — but did that make him Major League Baseball material? Save for a few pitchers, none of his countrymen had ever crossed the Pacific and earned steady work in the major leagues. Ichiro was just a wisp of a fel-

low, 5-foot-9, 160 pounds soaking wet, a snack for the pitching piranhas of the American League. Mr. Clemens and Mr. Martinez licked their chops. *Welcome to America, Mr. Ichiro. You need a haircut — we'll be happy to buzz you. Where would you like this fastball — in the ear or in the ribs?*

It didn't happen that way at all. The 27-year-old Ichiro joined the Seattle Mariners in 2001, quickly became their right fielder and leadoff hitter, and put on a season-long clinic on how to play the game with speed, finesse, cun-

MOST HITS IN A SEASON

PLAYER	TEAM	YEAR	HITS	GAMES	BA
GEORGE SISLER	ST. LOUIS BROWNS	1920	257	154	.407
LEFTY O'DOUL	PHILADELPHIA PHILLIES	1929	254	154	.398
BILL TERRY	NEW YORK GIANTS	1930	254	154	.401
AL SIMMONS	PHILADELPHIA ATHLETICS	1925	253	153	.384
ROGERS HORNSBY	ST. LOUIS CARDINALS	1922	250	154	.401
CHUCK KLEIN	PHILADELPHIA PHILLIES	1930	250	156	.386
TY COBB	DETROIT TIGERS	1911	248	146	.420
GEORGE SISLER	ST. LOUIS BROWNS	1922	246	141	.420
ICHIRO	SEATTLE MARINERS	2001	242	157	.350
BABE HERMAN	BROOKLYN DODGERS	1930	241	153	.393
HEINIE MANUSH	ST. LOUIS BROWNS	1928	241	154	.378
WADE BOGGS	BOSTON RED SOX	1985	240	161	.368
JESSE BURKETT	CLEVELAND SPIDERS	1896	240	133	.410
DARIN ERSTAD	ANAHEIM ANGELS	2000	240	157	.355

Ichiro's awestruck teammates dubbed him "Wizard,"
AND HIS BAT WAS A MAGIC WAND.

A Gold Glove and a Silver Slugger were among the spoils of success for Ichiro in his rookie season. Mariners president Chuck Armstrong presented the awards.

ning and daring. He fit right in — right in the double-knit 1970s that is, when baseball was played on carpet and in the fast lane, when one-hoppers into the gap became rabbit races, before the game muscled up and turned into Home Run Derby. Ichiro's awestruck teammates dubbed him "Wizard," and his bat was a magic wand. Not only could he seemingly make contact at will, he seemed able to spray the ball wherever he wished. He was so fast to first base that his grounders and choppers not struck directly at an infielder brought the crowd to its feet, straining to see if he would be safe. From right field, he tracked fly balls effortlessly and threw as strong and as true as anyone. Ichiro became a cult figure, so revered and recognized that he received more fan votes than anyone else for the All-Star Game. People soon referred to him only by his given name, dropping Suzuki, as if he were a rock star, South

"Don't you think that kids will think they can play in the big leagues
NOW THAT THEY'VE SEEN SOMEONE LIKE ME MAKE IT?"
— ICHIRO

American soccer player or professional wrestler. He became the only player in Major League Baseball that had his given name rather than his surname on his uniform jersey.

The Mariners hitched their wagon to this ball-playing phenomenon and achieved one of the greatest seasons in history, winning 116 games, equaling the most ever, before the fog rolled in and they stumbled in the playoffs against the mighty Yankees. For his part, Ichiro led the major leagues in bat-

ting average (.350) and stolen bases (56); got more hits (242) than anyone in 71 years, including an American League record 192 singles; and was first player since 1980 with three hitting streaks of 15 games or more. L surprise that he became the second man to be voted the Rookie of the Y and the Most Valuable Player in the same season. Ichiro had stirred the Ma League Baseball melting pot like few before him had, and he stretched game's boundaries across a deep, blue sea.

(1934)
CARL HUBBELL
STRIKES OUT BABE RUTH, LOU GEHRIG, JIMMIE FOXX, AL SIMMONS AND JOE CRONIN IN SUCCESSION IN THE ALL-STAR GAME

Carl Hubbell was a slightly built man, carrying about 170 pounds on his 6-foot frame.

HIS MOST STRIKING PHYSICAL TRAIT WAS HIS LEFT ARM,

which appeared to be deformed, twisted almost 180 degrees so the palm faced away from his body.

It was a self-induced abnormality, and for Hubbell a small price to pay

FOR A GLORIOUS CAREER IN THE MAJOR LEAGUES.

Hubbell's left arm turned inside out during 16 seasons of pitching for the New York Giants. His specialty pitch was a screwball, which is thrown with a violent snap of the wrist away from the body. Thrown properly, the pitch breaks in to left-handed batters and away from right-handers. Few, if any pitchers ever mastered the difficult screwball as well as Hubbell did. He did not throw exceptionally hard, yet he dominated hitters with his screwball, a superb curveball, uncanny control, and a steely nerve. "Emotions, if he has any, never affected him," another player once remarked.

Hubbell's achievement included five consecutive 20-win seasons and a record 24-game victory streak. He ranks with Lefty Grove, Whitey Ford, Sandy Koufax, Warren Spahn, Eddie Plank and Steve Carlton as the greatest left-handed pitchers of all time. Yet Hubbell largely is known for one amazing feat: His performance in the 1934 All-Star Game, when he struck out five consecutive batters in the first two innings.

These were no ordinary All-Stars: Babe Ruth, Lou Gehrig, Jimmie Foxx, Al Simmons, and Joe Cronin. All five are in the Hall of Fame, yet during a 30-minute span on the afternoon of July 10, 1934, in the Polo Grounds, his home turf, the 31-year-old Hubbell sent each one trudging back to the dugout, Louisville Slugger in tow.

The great sportswriter Grantland Rice was at the game and had this to say in his newspaper the following day: "The main glory went to the Carthage Catapault.... It was Carl Owen Hubbell, of Carthage, Missouri, who rode the skyline and earned the vocalistic uprising of about 50,000 fans. This great crowd paid its tribute to a stout heart, a keen brain, and a great left arm when Carl Hubbell struck out Babe Ruth, Lou Gehrig, Jimmie Foxx, Al Simmons, and Joe Cronin in succession through the first and second innings with a baffling assortment of curves, screwballs and zigzags that stood five of baseball's greatest hitters on their well-known heads."

Hubbell began the game inauspiciously, yielding a single and a walk. Then came Ruth, who took a called third strike. Gehrig struck out chasing a darting screwball, then offered this advice as he and Foxx passed each other: "You might as well cut. It won't get any higher." Foxx struck out on three successive screwballs. Simmons and Cronin soon would follow, each just as helpless as the preceding three against the Hubbell screwball. Bill Dickey broke the spell with a single, then Hubbell struck out his counterpart, Lefty Gomez. It was Cronin who years later put the feat in perspective. "I was the star of that group," he said. "I was the only one who got a foul off him."

Fernando Valenzuela of the Los Angeles Dodgers, another left-handed screwball master, matched Hubbell's feat 52 years later in the 1986 All-Star Game. But only one of Valenzuela's victims, Cal Ripken Jr., is likely to make the Hall of Fame.

CONSECUTIVE STRIKEOUTS IN THE ALL★STAR GAME

1934 CARL HUBBELL NEW YORK GIANTS

	AVG.	HR	K/AB
* BABE RUTH NEW YORK YANKEES	.342	714	.158
* LOU GEHRIG NEW YORK YANKEES	.340	493	.099
* JIMMIE FOXX PHILADELPHIA ATHLETICS	.325	534	.161
* AL SIMMONS CHICAGO WHITE SOX	.334	307	.084
* JOE CRONIN WASHINGTON SENATORS	.301	170	.092

1986 FERNANDO VALENZUELA LOS ANGELES DODGERS

	AVG.	HR	K/AB
DON MATTINGLY NEW YORK YANKEES	.307	222	.063
CAL RIPKEN JR. BALTIMORE ORIOLES	.276	431	.113
JESSE BARFIELD TORONTO BLUE JAYS	.256	241	.259
LOU WHITAKER DETROIT TIGERS	.276	244	.128
TEDDY HIGUERA MILWAUKEE BREWERS	—	—	—

1999 PEDRO MARTINEZ BOSTON RED SOX

	AVG.	HR	K/AB
BARRY LARKIN CINCINNATI REDS	.299	181	.101
LARRY WALKER COLORADO ROCKIES	.315	309	.176
SAMMY SOSA CHICAGO CUBS	.277	450	.261
MARK McGWIRE ST. LOUIS CARDINALS	.263	583	.258

STATISTICS ARE CAREER TOTALS THROUGH 2001 | HIGUERA DID NOT BAT IN 213 REGULAR-SEASON GAMES; HIS ONLY AT BAT WAS IN THE 1986 ALL-STAR GAME | ★ HALL OF FAME